COLONEL HANS CHRISTIAN HEG
and the
NORWEGIAN AMERICAN EXPERIENCE

COLONEL HANS CHRISTIAN HEG

and the

NORWEGIAN AMERICAN EXPERIENCE

ODD S. LOVOLL

MINNESOTA
HISTORICAL
SOCIETY PRESS

mnhspress.org

The Minnesota Historical Society Press is a member of the Association of University Presses.

Manufactured in the United States of America.

10 9 8 7 6 5 4 3 2 1

♾ The paper used in this publication meets the minimum requirements of the American National Standard for Information Sciences—Permanence for Printed Library Materials, ANSI Z39.48-1984.

International Standard Book Number

ISBN: 978-1-68134-250-4 (paper)
ISBN: 978-1-68134-251-1 (e-book)

Library of Congress Control Number: 2022950120

This and other Minnesota Historical Society Press books are available from popular e-book vendors.

To

LUKAS *and* PHOEBE ANN

Contents

Preface

On June 23, 2020, in Madison, Wisconsin, demonstrations by protestors, enraged by the arrest of a Black man, turned violent. The memorial statue of Colonel Hans Christian Heg that stood on the capitol grounds was beheaded and thrown into Lake Monona. The words "Black is beautiful" were spray-painted on the statue. Two protestors interviewed by *Wisconsin State Journal* claimed that vandalizing the statue was intended to draw attention to their view of Wisconsin as a racially unjust state. Their actions created renewed interest in Colonel Heg's life story and legacy as a Union soldier and abolitionist.

The following day, *Aftenposten*, Norway's leading newspaper—under the heading "The Norwegian American Fought Against Slavery. Tonight the Statue of Him Was Torn Down, 'Beheaded' and Thrown into the River"—published a long article about Heg and the destruction of the statue, stressing the paradox of dishonoring the memory of a Civil War hero like Colonel Heg. The story became front-page news in both Norway and the United States. The statue was restored and rededicated on May 29, 2022.

Before these dramatic events, James T. Heg, Colonel Heg's great-great-grandson, had encouraged me to consider writing Heg's biography. At that time, James Heg served as deputy chief of mission at the

US embassy in Oslo, Norway. My own longtime interest in Heg and in the formative years of Norwegian immigration, chronicled in my book *The Promise of America*, published in 1984, convinced me that the attack on the Heg statue demanded biographical documentation of Colonel Heg's journey through life, brief as it turned out to be.

Many historians of Norwegian immigration have focused exclusively on the final destination. The immigrants more or less simply appear on the American shore. Historical narratives frequently neglect the subjects of the immigrants' homeland, as well as their lengthy and hazardous Atlantic crossings on sailing ships. The legacy of the homeland's social environment, religious and civic traditions, and the circumstances that encouraged emigration are all essential constituents in a Norwegian immigrant's biography. They clarify how newcomers accepted and adjusted to a land greatly different from the one they had left behind. Sections of the first chapter of this book are consequently devoted to defining local peculiarities and traditions of Norwegian heritage—including the beauty of the local landscape—that accompanied individual immigrants as they sought a new life in America.

The central focus of the biography is on Hans Christian Heg and his family, as it must be; the intent, however, is to place the narrative in a broad historical and social context. There was the hardship of life on the American frontier and in the pioneer Muskego settlement, where Hans Heg's father, Even Heg, played a strong role as leader, as Even also had done in Lier, his home in Norway. The personal life of Hans Heg, his marriage to Gunild Heg, and the care of their children represent an important aspect of the story. There was as well his youthful search for gold in California. Heg was an ardent member of the Free Soil Party and joined the Republican Party shortly after it was formed. He enjoyed a notable career in local and state politics and served as Wisconsin state prison commissioner. His accomplishments as a rising young politician are well documented.

Hans Heg was an outspoken antislavery activist. Heg's appointment by Governor Alexander Randall as colonel of the Fifteenth Wisconsin Volunteer Regiment, the Norwegian Regiment, made military service a national engagement and gave him a heroic status. The final two chapters, about Heg and the Fifteenth in the Civil War, are intended to relate Heg's life and wartime experience rather than give a traditional military history. Heg consistently displayed a respectful and involved regard in his relationships, a characteristic made evident when he served as prison commissioner. His devotion to his family is manifest in his correspondence with Gunild, and also in his letters to his son, Edmund, and his daughter, Hilda, in which his Civil War engagement was a regular topic. Colonel Hans Christian Heg gave his life on the battlefield at Chickamauga. He left a lasting legacy.

CHAPTER 1

The Norwegian Homeland

Two Centennials

The American Civil War created heroes. The most famous among Norwegian Americans was undoubtedly Colonel Hans Christian Heg of the Fifteenth Wisconsin Volunteer Regiment. Consisting almost entirely of Norwegians, the regiment itself became a symbol and source of great ethnic pride. This esteem was manifested at the centennial Seventeenth of May celebration in May 1914 at the Minnesota State Fairgrounds when Norwegians in the Twin Cities arranged a grand festival to commemorate Norway's liberal national constitution adopted at Eidsvoll on May 17, 1814. Norway was reborn as a nation after several centuries of political and cultural subjection to Denmark. At the 1914 celebration survivors of the Fifteenth Wisconsin Regiment in attendance attracted special attention. Twenty-two of the twenty-six gray-haired veterans responded to the roll call by Lieutenant Nils J. Gilbert of Company A, Fifteenth Wisconsin Regiment, and assembled in the Old Settlers' Log Cabin on the fairgrounds. A grandstand rally rendered emotional homage to surviving Civil War veterans. At this, their last major reunion, the twenty-two veterans adopted a resolution which in part stated their "heartfelt and respectful greetings to the Norwegian people, with wishes that God will

At the centennial celebration at the Minnesota state fairgrounds on May 17, 1914, A. E. Rice of Willmar, a veteran of the Fifteenth Wisconsin volunteers, held up the regimental flag carried through three years of fighting.
Minneapolis Tribune, May 19, 1914, 8

protect old Norway, its King, Parliament, and people." Newspapers in Norway printed the resolution.[1]

Similarly, the Norse-American Centennial in 1925 was a significant undertaking. Norwegian forces united around the celebration of the centennial of the first Norwegian group immigration, the dramatic voyage of the sloop *Restauration*, which departed from Stavanger, Norway, on July 4, 1825, and landed in New York harbor on October 9. The main celebration took place, like the one in 1914, on the fairgrounds between Minneapolis and St. Paul, lasting from June 6 to 9, 1925. An impressive centennial pageant with more than a thousand actors in twenty-four scenes concluded the festivities. Fifteen thousand people attended. The *Minneapolis Journal* in its June 7, 1925, issue had the following long heading: "Centennial Pageant, With 1,500 in cast, to Show Trials, Adventures of Norse Pioneers. Scenes Cover Whole Life 'of Typical Immigrants, with Folklore, Witches, Fairies, Indian Battles, Politics, Civil War' as Settings."

The *St. Paul News* reported on May 13, 1925, that S. H. Holstad, managing director of the centennial committee, had announced that—after a countrywide search—Carl Nelson of Milwaukee, Wisconsin, ninety-six years old, was entitled to the honor of being the oldest living Norse-American veteran of the Civil War. In recognition of that distinction the committee selected Nelson to attend the centennial celebration as an honored guest. The journal explained that Nelson "served in Co. F. 15th Wisconsin Infantry, of which Col. Hans Heg, killed at Chickamauga, was the commander." The centennial pageant centered on the biography of Colonel Hans Christian Heg, from his childhood in Norway to his life and military service in America. Norwegians feted the hero of the Civil War with great enthusiasm. In the program Heg was described as "the type of all that is best and noblest in a citizen."

In 1925, at the Minnesota state fairgrounds, descendants of Norwegian immigrants posed in front of a full-size replica of the small sloop *Restauration*, built that year for the Norse-American Centennial celebration in Minneapolis. The original brought the first boatload of Norwegian immigrants to America in 1825. Minnesota Historical Society

These two centennials celebrated heroic historical ventures in the homeland and among Norwegians in America. "Commemorative celebrations," as Carl Chrislock states, "have been a significant component of the Norwegian American way of life." In the 1920s May 17 festivals asserted the value of a Norwegian American heritage and a Norwegian national background—indeed, while showing loyalty to the new homeland, they protested against strong American nativism during World War I. Heg's legacy and that of the Fifteenth Wisconsin

Regiment are evocative manifestations of how Norwegian Americans established an important and acceptable version of their past as immigrant citizens. Their place in American society and history is decisive.

Two families constitute a central part of the narrative that follows. Their history exemplifies the challenges of adjustment as well as the influence immigrants have on the culture as well as on the evolving social and fiscal growth of a new society. The story of Hans Christian Heg and family begins in Lier in Buskerud province (*amt*), where Heg was born on December 21, 1829, at Haugestad in the village of Lierbyen. Gunild (Gunhild) Einong (Einung), who became his wife in America, was born on December 30, 1833, on the Einung family farm in Mæl parish in the municipality of Tinn in Telemark province.[2]

HISTORIC LIER

The municipality (*kommune*) of Lier borders the city of Drammen to the southwest and west. Lierbyen is the administrative center of Lier. The village is located on the Lierelva River in the broad and well-farmed Lierdalen, the Lier valley, which extends from the Drammensfjord north toward Sylling near Lake Tyrifjorden. It is encircled on both sides of the valley by wooded hillsides. The valley is relatively densely populated at present, the growth related to nearby Drammen and Oslo. There are several villages in the municipality, the largest being Tranby. Lier enjoys a diverse economy.

But Lier in the mid-1800s in terms of population and livelihoods was historically quite different. Strong population growth both nationally and in individual communities was the basis of nineteenth-century social change. Norway's population more than doubled between 1769 and 1865. The issue: What would become of all the new people in an economy mostly limited to agriculture? Would all of them acquire a farm or land to cultivate? In 1845, according to a

Lierdalen, the Lier Valley, showing Lierbyen and the valley's fertile farmland.
Photo by Knut Anders Andersen

history of Lier, more than one-third of the population was branded
as poor. It was a typical agricultural community with land-owning
farmers, cotters (*husmenn*), and hired laborers. The social distinctions
were obvious. In eastern Norway the divide between the wealthy
freeholding farmer and his cotters was insurmountable; in compari-
son, western Norway, with its smaller independent farms, had greater
social equality.

In a history of Lier that regularly focuses on individual *liunger* (residents of Lier), Rolf Fladby gives an explicit picture of life there at the
time under consideration, but also indicates some improvements
in agriculture, forestry, and "a dawning industry." "Even though,"
according to Fladby, "circumstances for many were poor throughout

this period, an ever so little betterment may, to be sure, be noticed from the middle of the [nineteenth] century."

The fertile farmland and better farming methods benefited the owners of large farms, of which there were some, Fladby explains; but also the owners of middle-sized and small farms might little by little notice some advancement in living standards. There were many mouths to feed, however, regularly a large family, but also the aging parents of the inheritor of the ancestral farm. The system termed *kår* or *føderåd* required a pension to be paid to the former farm owner after cession to heirs, generally son (*odelsgutt*) to father.

Official national reports on agriculture document the progress made during the first half of the nineteenth century. The report for 1835 praises Lier for improvement in farming equipment as well as for changing to new grain species. The hay crop had by 1835 also improved a little. On the other hand, little progress in cattle breeding could be found, perhaps because in some places no summer pasture existed. Other sources show that *liunger* tried new ways of livestock breeding; a mixture of English and Spanish sheep made their entrance into the community. The more traditional smaller, wool-producing sheep could still be seen in mountain regions. The economy and livelihoods were based on agriculture to a high degree during the relevant historical period—though there was clear evidence of changes to come.

The cotter class had an inferior social status. The system of cotters (*husmenn*) in eastern Norway had many common traits. A cotter rented a dwelling and a parcel of land from the farm owner with a contractual agreement to work as a farmhand. This work requirement, for which there was some compensation, secured farm labor for the owner and was perhaps the most characteristic of the cotter system. The terms were hard, and living conditions for the cotter and his family might be quite miserable; both wife and young children needed to find employment in the community to make ends meet. The average annual salary for farmhands in the 1840s, according to the monetary system in place from 1816 to 1875, was for men twenty-four to twenty-five *speciedaler* and for women twelve to thirteen. Day workers made about twelve to sixteen *skilling* and fare daily. A *speciedaler* equaled 120 *skilling*. The fare varied greatly. Fladby cites documents showing that servants simply ran away because of malnutrition.

A national poor relief system was in place. The protocols of the poor relief commission give insight into the situation in Lier. People paid a fixed poor relief tax, in commodity or currency. According to Fladby, a substantial number of poor relief recipients belonged to the cotter class. Their last names ending in -*eie* (possession), such as Brastadeie, identified them as cotters. Some of those on poor relief contributed to their own subsistence in addition to the poor relief subsidy, but most belonged to the group of paupers identified as "burdensome poor" (*byrdefulle fattige*). They were regularly "rented out" (*bortleid*) to the lowest bidder. Fladby quotes from the 1838 commission's report the following: "The very burdensome paupers (*huslegder*) were today lodged with the lowest bidders." How they fared is a difficult question, and one not of much interest to the authorities, Fladby states. There was, however, some supervision so that the lodgers did not suffer direct maltreatment. Many lodging children experienced abuse, especially those who had lost their mothers.[3]

The decade of the 1860s is generally regarded as the culmination of the cotter age. Thereafter the number of cotters and cotter's farms declined rapidly. Emigration to America is often given as an important cause for the liquidation of the cotter system. But there were also transformative changes in Norwegian agriculture and increasing opportunities in Norway's expanding urban centers. In any case, the cotters and their children left for America or made a living outside of agriculture in the homeland. The small cotter farmsteads were empty, and there was a shortage of workers in the countryside.

Heg(g) and Hegsbro were the original designations of the Lierbyen locality. The Lier railroad station on the line between Drammen-Christiania (Oslo), with connecting roads in different directions, opened in 1872 and made the depot a central location. "Lier station" or simply Lier gradually replaced the old names. People settled in the section around the station. The area was built up with villas and businesses, including Lier Dairy, and gained an "urban" appearance. In 1904 the municipal board moved to Hegsbro from Nordal, where it had held its meetings since about 1850. Nordal had a *skysstasjon*, a station for traveling by horse, and was a central point in Lier until about 1880 and the arrival of the railroad. It was a place of communal and other meetings, concerts, and May 17 arrangements. The name Lierbyen came into use only shortly before 1920.[4]

THE HEG FAMILY

The story begins at the farm Ødegård in Rygge south of the city of Moss in the province of Østfold, at that time Smaalenenes *amt*, where Even Hansen Ødegården was born June 17, 1789. Judging from his many endeavors and achievements, he must have been both ambitious and persistent in his challenging pursuits, both in Norway and later in America. In 1824 he moved to Hurum, located on the peninsula between the Oslofjord and the Drammensfjord. He made it to Heg in Lier in 1825. In the nineteenth century, and even later, it was common to adopt a farm name (*gårdsnavn*), both to indicate place of residence and as a surname. Even Hansen Ødegården consequently took the name Even Hansen Heg.

An old inn (*gjestgiveri*) in Heg dated back to the 1700s; from the late 1820s Even Hansen Heg maintained and operated it. He made a living as an innkeeper and as the owner of a local general country store (*landhandleri*). Heg even opened Lier's first small library. He was subject to a special poor relief tax in order to serve hard liquor. In 1838 he paid twenty-five *speciedaler* to the relief fund in Lier, indicating both status and economic success. It was the highest tax paid by anyone in Lier in similar business enterprise. Theodore C. Blegen describes Heg as "a shrewd and prosperous innkeeper."

On April 17, 1827, Even Heg married Siri (Sigrid) Olsdatter Kallerud Heg, born on October 21, 1799, on the Kallerud farm in Flesberg in the Numedal region of Buskerud, owned by her parents Ole Gullixsen and Anne Olsdatter Kallerud. Forestry and agriculture dominated the Flesberg economy.

They were married at the Frogner church, the main Lutheran sanctuary in Lier. The church was consecrated on November 1, 1694. An earlier church, destroyed by lightning, had existed at the same location from the 1100s, perhaps, as Per Otto Borgen suggests, where there had been a pagan ceremonial site. It is all reminiscent of Lier's long and rich history.

Their son Hans Christian Heg was born at Christmastime in 1829. He was baptized at the Frogner church. Three more children were born in the Heg family, Ole Heg (1831–1911), Andrea Heg (1835–1880), and Sophie Heg (1837–1921). Even Heg was a devout follower of the teachings of Hans Nielsen Hauge (1771–1824), "the apostle of Norwegian pietism." Heg was a good friend of Tollef Bache (1770–1848), the area's leading Haugean. Bache was a Norwegian farmer, businessman, and lay preacher. He served as sheriff (*lensmann*) in Uvdal and Nore in the Numedal valley from 1796. The following year he converted and in 1799 met with Hans Nielsen Hauge. Bache thereafter for a period became a lay preacher; at a revival meeting at Pentecost in 1800 at Ål parish in the Hallingdal district of Buskerud, Bache was confronted by the Lutheran pastor and the sheriff and arrested and jailed, even though he himself still was a sheriff. Bache was released by paying bail and, after lengthy legal proceedings, was acquitted the following year. Bache had a good head for business, and encouraged by Hauge, he moved to Drammen in 1802 and became a well-to-do lumber merchant. His home in Drammen was a center for Haugeanism.

The Haugeans did not leave the Norwegian Lutheran state church but worked for a renewal of Norwegian Christian life within its framework. The pietistic movement that came out of the Haugean revival had a profound impact on both secular and religious history in Norway. It became a folk movement that defied authority and the dominance of officials and the privileged classes; a growing class consciousness stimulated members of the rural population to enter into politics. Hans Nielsen Hauge was himself of peasant stock and had little formal education. He violated the Conventicle Act of 1741 (*Konventikkelplakaten*), which prohibited any religious meetings not authorized by the Church of Norway. Only ordained ministers could administer the sacraments. Hauge advocated a priesthood of all believers and thus challenged the authority of the Lutheran ministry. Hauge faced state persecution because of the religious revivals he inspired on his travels throughout much of Norway and was imprisoned no fewer than fourteen times, spending a total of nine years in prison.

The Haugean religious revivals coincided with the emigration to America. Paragraph two in the otherwise liberal (for the time) democratic Norwegian Constitution adopted May 17, 1814, stipulated that the Evangelical Lutheran religion would be the state's official religion in Norway, and "Inhabitants confessing to it are obligated to rear their children in the same." In addition it denied adherents of certain faiths access to the kingdom. The prejudicial final sentence in paragraph two reads: "Jesuits and monastic orders must not be tolerated. Jews are still excluded." In 1845, following sharp dispute and great suspense, Norway's parliament, the Storting (Grand Assembly), passed the religious dissenter act guaranteeing religious freedom. Only in 1851, however, was the exclusion of Jews nullified. Prejudice against non-Lutherans persisted. Early immigrants left behind these biased religious circumstances in Norway. They transitioned "from the authoritarian episcopally organized Lutheran state church with automatic membership in Norway to an extreme free-church system based on voluntarism." The Haugean faith had considerable influence on the institutional history of Norwegian American Lutheranism.

The Hegs, like most Haugeans, were inspired not only by Hauge's spiritual message as a lay preacher but also by his message within commerce. Haugeans were encouraged to launch shipyards, paper mills, textile industries, and other initiatives; economic strength would make Hauge's followers more independent. Hauge combined economics and Christian morals, including modesty, honesty, and hard work. In addition to the many ventures undertaken by Even Heg and family, they also joined edifying Haugean religious meetings. The inn, their main place of work, was by all accounts a bustling and demanding business enterprise. Military drill grounds were located on the flat fields just south of the building. The officers stationed there were among the regular guests served at the inn. One can only speculate how it all affected Hans Christian, then only a child. A folder published by the historical society in Lier has the following conjecture: "We know nothing about the boy's adolescence at Heg. But we have to assume that early on he had to do his part in regard to the easier tasks at the inn, have responsibility for his younger siblings, and take part in his parents' religious activity. Association with hardy and brawny officers and impressions from the drill grounds must surely also have made an impression on him and would have consequences many years later."[5]

Tinn in Telemark

Telemark province (*fylke*) was known as Bratsberg *amt* before 1918. The municipality of Tinn is located in the northwestern corner of the province. The town of Rjukan is the administrative center. Tinn borders on Buskerud province to the north and east, and to the west it extends into the vast Hardanger mountain plateau (Hardangervidda). Tinn is a distinctive mountain district. According to Andres A. Svalestuen's insightful and detailed master's thesis on the emigration from Tinn, merely 0.6 percent of the total surface of the municipality is currently under cultivation, while 99 percent consists of upland pastures, mountainous terrain, forests, and numerous lakes.

Nearly 90 percent of the total area lies 2,625 feet or more above sea level; the large inland lake Tinnsjø, at 630 feet (188 meters) above sea level, is the low point, and the highest mountain peak is Gaustatoppen, 6,178 feet (1,883 meters) above sea level. Five valleys spread out from the northern part of lake Tinnsjø. During the era under consideration, rivers and high waterfalls rushed through these valleys. There were small farms along the river valleys and up the mountain slopes, often located on steep inclines with an average of only five to seven and a half acres cultivated. Field crops played a minor part in agriculture. Cattle raising or dairying combined with forestry characterized the farmers' livelihoods.

The social layers in Tinn included the cotter system, and, as was the case in Lier, it expanded in the early nineteenth century. The lowered death rate and a higher birth rate rapidly increased the number of people without property. An agricultural economy with bounded available acreage could not absorb or accommodate the rapid population growth, and this reality brought about change in the community's social composition. The percentage of landowning farmers consequently decreased from 56 percent of the population

Gaustatoppen (The Gausta Summit) in Tinn in Telemark, a distinctive mountain district. From the summit an extensive portion of Norway's mainland is visible. Photo by John Wroughton

in 1801 to only 43 percent by 1835. The number of landless cotters and cotters with land increased substantially in percentage of the population, and even more so the number of day laborers and farmworkers. In addition many people were on public relief and officially classified as poor. As Svalestuen concludes, the agrarian society in Tinn was clearly producing a growing proletariat. The danger of merging into this class "undoubtedly spurred many young people on to test fortune somewhere else."[6]

THE EINUNG FAMILY

The Nord Einung farm was located in Mæl parish in Upper Telemark in sight of Gaustatoppen. The owners of the farm from the 1780s were Ola Høljesson Einung and Susanne Øysteinsdatter Miland. They had many children, but only Gunhild Olsdatter, born in 1794, and Jakob Olsen, born in 1799, lived to adulthood. Ola Høljesson died in 1818, Susanne died eight years earlier, and Gunhild inherited the farm. In 1822 Jakob married Anne Jonsdatter Såheim, born in 1798 at Såheim, a small farm once part of a larger farm, also located in Tinn. *Tinn Soga* observed that Jakob "supposedly was not great looking and Anne would likely have preferred a different boy." As the story goes, she even chanted her wishes just before she married Jakob. These details highlight their humanity.

Anne and Jakob acquired the Nord Einung farm by purchasing it from Jakob's sister for 166 *speciedaler*. By the time of the ownership transfer Nord Einung was held to be a good farm. In 1835 they sowed two and a half barrels of barley and four barrels of potatoes and reared eight cattle (*storfe*) and fifteen sheep (*småfe*). The Einungs had eight children, five daughters and three sons. Their daughter Gunild (Gunhild) was born on December 10, 1833. They owned the Einung farm until 1842, when the family immigrated to America.[7]

THE LIER AND TINN STORY

In 1931 historian Theodore C. Blegen published his groundbreaking work *Norwegian Migration to America, 1825–1860*. The years 1825 to 1865 are generally defined as the founding phase of Norwegian immigration to America. This bigger picture will be dealt with more fully in the final section of this chapter, as we place the movement from Lier and Tinn in a broader historical context.

The Heg family was well informed about movement to America from its early stages. In the 1830s Drammen became a center of emigration interest. Residents of Lier, in close vicinity, were also much engaged in discussing opportunities abroad. As early as 1824 *Drammens Tidende* published a series of descriptive articles on America, a land "for the present and future." Social and economic circumstances at home opened people to seeking a better life outside the

homeland. Blegen notes that in 1825 two men, Peder B. Smith and
Hans E. Hjorth, left Drammen and settled in White County, Indiana,
where they had land and owned a sawmill.

That same year, on July 4, 1825, the sailing of the small sloop
Restauration from Stavanger on the southwestern coast of Norway
marked a dramatic beginning of Norwegian emigration in the nineteenth century. The sloop followed a circuitous route, traveling as far
south as the harbor of Funchal in Madeira, and did not arrive at New
York until October 9, more than three months after leaving Stavanger. The *New York Daily Advertiser* for October 15, 1825, described the
party of strangers from a distant nation in a vessel not well suited to
cross the stormy Atlantic as "A Novel Sight."

There were fifty-two persons on board the sloop, crew and passengers, who all intended to emigrate. During their long voyage a child
was born. In Norwegian American history they are referred to as the
Sloopers, and their arrival, as conveyed earlier, was later celebrated
by Norwegian Americans. Most of the Sloopers came from rural communities in the province of Rogaland, especially from the municipality of Tysvær, and a few were from Stavanger. Cleng Peerson, at
various times called "the father of Norwegian emigration," served as
their advance agent and, after investigating conditions in America,
returned to Norway the summer of 1824 to report on his findings.
He shortly went back to America to prepare for the Sloopers' arrival.

A strong religious motivation made the pioneer emigration unique
and has overshadowed the economic concerns that also influenced
the decision to emigrate. Lars Larsen Geilane, a declared Quaker and
a member of the Society of Friends in Stavanger, led the group; many
of the other Sloopers sympathized with Quakerism and converted
after their arrival in America. Haugeans made up a second group
among the emigrants, designated as "the holy." The two groups were
brought together by a shared pietistic conviction, an experience of

conversion, and their opposition to authorities and the powerful and religiously monopolistic position of the Norwegian Lutheran state church. They sought religious freedom and the right of lay people to preach the Word of God.

Assisted by American Quakers the Sloopers moved to northern New York State near Lake Ontario on land Cleng Peerson had bought, which became known as the Kendall settlement. It formed a beachhead, a point of contact, in the New World. However, most of the Sloopers, along with newcomers from Norway in the mid-1830s, established the Fox River settlement in the Fox River valley in Illinois, about seventy miles southwest of the frontier community of Chicago, which became an important destination for Norwegian immigrants.

The pioneer sailing of the *Restauration* played an important role in the early movement from both Lier and Tinn as well as from Norway in general. The arrival of news about America became a prime factor in the spread of immigration. In the years after 1825, especially in the early thirties, people ventured to America. Their correspondence, the so-called "America letters," supplied knowledge of America, as did missives from visiting Norwegian Americans. The letters Gjert Gregoriussen Hovland sent home after coming to Kendall in 1831 circulated widely in Norway and created interest in America. He described the "pleasant and fertile land" and the greater freedom of America. The poor harvests in Norway at that time made people receptive to the favorable information.

In the summer of 1836 two brigs, *Den norske klippe* and *Norden*, sailed from Stavanger with a total of 167 people destined for America, introducing annual immigration. Knud Andersen Slogvig, who like Hovland had emigrated in 1831, had returned to Norway the previous year and served as leader for the emigrants on board *Norden*. His return greatly influenced emigration from the west coast provinces of Rogaland, where Stavanger is located, and Hordaland farther north.[8]

The brothers Ole Nattestad and Ansten Nattestad from Veggli in Numedal had an important role in the early exodus. In 1836 they crossed the mountain to the west coast on a trading venture. In Tysvær they learned about America and were gripped by the idea of leaving to seek new opportunities in the west. They brought America letters with them back to Tinn. The brothers left for America the spring of 1837. That same year a group of fifty-six people from Tinn embarked on their hazardous journey to America on May 17. They secured passage in Gothenburg on the Swedish brig *Niord* and reached New York on August 15. As the first group of emigrants from eastern Norway, their move was a notable historical event.

Drammen was a center of emigration interest in the 1830s. In the spring of 1838 Ansten Nattestad returned to Norway by way of New Orleans and Liverpool. He carried with him the manuscripts of two books, one by Ole Nattestad published in Drammen in 1839 titled *Beskrivelse over en Reise til Nordamerica* (Description of a Journey to North America). In this rare document Ole Nattestad gave a full account of his and Ansten's departure from Gothenburg on May 11, 1837, on the ship *Hilda*, a large vessel with a cargo of iron. It made the crossing to Fall River, Massachusetts, in only thirty-two days. From there the brothers made their way inland to distant Illinois.

The second manuscript was by Ole Rynning, who had emigrated from Snåsa in North Trøndelag the spring of 1837. He crossed on the bark *Ægir*, which departed from Bergen on April 7, arriving in New York on June 9, with eighty-four passengers, mostly from the region surrounding the city; except for Rynning and a second passenger they were all of the peasant class. Rynning became the party's leader and spokesman. Rynning's father was the parish minister in Snåsa and a man of considerable distinction. Rynning became an outstanding figure in the history of Norwegian immigration. His book, *Sandfærdig Beretning om Amerika til Oplysning og Nytte for Bonde og Menigmand*

(True Account of America for the Enlightenment and Benefit of the Peasant and the Common Man), was brought out in Christiania (Oslo) in 1838. This guidebook or "America book" was significant in augmenting the Norwegian overseas movement. Rynning's "influence," Blegen claims, "on the early Norwegian emigration was as great as that of Cleng Peerson and possibly greater."

In the spring of 1839 Ansten Nattestad led a party of more than 130 emigrants, most of them from Rollag, Veggli, and northern Numedal and some from Tinn and Heddal. They sailed from Drammen on June 12 on the *Emilie* and arrived in New York on August 22, after stopping in Gothenburg to pick up a cargo of iron bars, which they intended to sell in America. Even the Sloopers had transported a cargo of iron bars and plates on the small *Restauration* and hoped to realize a profit by selling them.

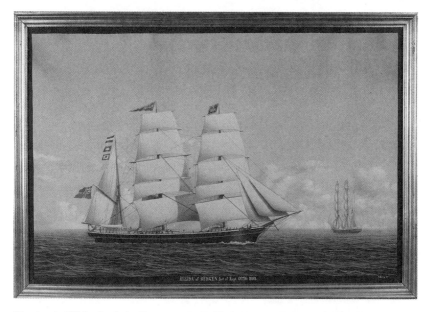

The bark *Ellida*, built in Bergen. © Fredrik Martin Sørvig 1868/Bergen Maritime Museum

An emigrant party under the leadership of John Nelson Luraas from Upper Telemark, mainly from Tinn and Hjartdal, came to play a primary role in establishing a Norwegian settlement on the shores of Muskego Lake in Waukesha County, Wisconsin. It was the beginning of one of the best-known Norwegian communities in the United States. Luraas was the eldest son on the family farm and thus an *odelsgutt*, the heir to a farm encumbered with substantial debt. He left in 1839, as he himself relates, because he saw no way of "buying out my sisters and brothers so that no injustice was done to them, and finally providing a pension for my father." This sort of situation could lead to emigration whether one was an elder or a younger son. Letters from earlier emigrants and Rynning's book convinced Luraas to emigrate. His group took passage in Gothenburg together with a party of emigrants from Stavanger and engaged an American captain whose ship, loaded with iron, was ready to sail for Massachusetts. After a voyage of nine weeks the Luraas emigrants landed in Boston and thereafter made their way west.[9]

To Wisconsin: The Hegs and the Einungs

Heg Immigration

The route by way of Gothenburg was in 1838 followed by several minor groups of emigrants. That year two good friends of the Hegs departed for America: Søren Bache, the son of Tollef Bache, the leading Haugean in Lier, and Johannes Johansen. They left on July 15, on the *Skogmand*, and arrived at Newport on September 2, the first stage of a journey that was to bear important fruit, as later recorded in Søren Bache's diary.

The Hegs were in close contact with the early stages of the exodus to America. They eagerly awaited letters from Bache and Johansen. Encouraged by positive reports about opportunities in America, Even Hansen Heg in the spring of 1840 sold his property and assumed leadership of a party of immigrants, including his wife, Siri Olsdatter Heg, and their four children; there were about thirty persons from Drammen and Lier and also a smaller group from Voss in western Norway.

They set sail from Drammen on May 17 on the *Emilie*, the same vessel in which the Nattestad party had crossed the Atlantic the year before. Like earlier groups, the Heg party secured a cargo of iron in Gothenburg. The emigrants experienced an eleven-week stormy voyage across the deep blue sea before they reached New York. The Heg party moved west by way of the Erie Canal, opened in 1825, linking Lake Erie at Buffalo with the Hudson River at Albany, a 363-mile waterway. From Buffalo they went by steamer on the Great Lakes to Milwaukee. This common route was also taken by earlier Norwegian immigrant parties, including the Sloopers when moving to the Fox River valley of Illinois. The emigrants from Voss continued to Chicago, the third Norwegian settlement in America; their fellow Vossings (immigrants from Voss) constituted a dominant element in that emerging Norwegian colony. Heg and most of those from Drammen headed for Muskego, which was Heg's objective. Among the latter was Ole K. Trovatten, who hailed from Telemark and who won fame as a writer of influential "America letters" and also an article in a journal where he recounted the Heg emigration.

Hans Christian, then only eleven years old, was, to cite Joseph Schafer in *The Wisconsin Blue Book*, "just the age to be impressed with the strange things seen on the voyage and in the new home." Growing up in a frontier community, Hans Christian experienced many of the central events in the pioneer history of the West. Heg and family were welcomed by Søren Bache and Johannes Johansen, who had visited the Muskego settlement but selected land on the shores of Wind Lake in what became Norway Township in Racine County. From this location they had promised, via letters back to Norway, that immigrants would find good land and favorable conditions in Wisconsin.[10]

Einung Immigration

Tinn was, as stated earlier, in 1837 the point of departure for the first emigrant group to leave eastern Norway, and through many decades it had a very high rate of emigration, relatively higher than most of the other communities in Telemark. It is not known what compelled Jakob Olsen Einung (the name in America revised to Einong) to emigrate, but apparently he was insistent. Family sources credit him with having great concern about the inheritance he could provide his children. The oldest son would inherit the Nord Einung property, leaving all the other children to make their own way in the world. In the new country, where good land was cheap, Jakob believed his children would have a better future. Indeed, upon arrival in Muskego, Jakob purchased forty acres of land for each of his children.

Anne Einung resisted immigration and was greatly uneasy about leaving her native land, a concern she shared with friends and relatives, predicting she would not survive the journey. In 1842 the family sold the Nord Einung farm; before leaving for America that summer, Anne was reported to have said, "I am not going for my own sake, but for the children. I will never get to America." The family secured accommodations on the immigrant sailing ship *Ellida*; it became a grievous voyage. The crossing, expected to last five or six weeks, extended to thirteen weeks because of storms and unfavorable winds. A shipboard epidemic of typhoid fever took the lives of Anne and her daughter Suzanne, twenty-one years old. Her prediction had come true.

Telesoga describes Jakob and the surviving children in great anguish and sorrow as they stand on the deck of *Ellida* by the sheet-wrapped bodies of Anne and Suzanne. A contemporary account states the following: "After allowing a moment for a final prayer, the sailors pick the shrouded bodies up and lower them with ropes and pulleys into the gray waves of the North Atlantic." This tragic and heart-breaking ritual was not all that unusual when crossing the Atlantic in the era of sailing ships. After landing in New York, the diminished Einung family made it safely across the Great Lakes and in the early fall of 1842 reached their destination in Wisconsin.[11]

THE FOUNDING PHASE OF IMMIGRATION

Emigration

The *Restauration*'s historic migration in 1825 established a contact with the New World—an essential component for the great exodus in

Conditions aboard sailing ships were crowded and unhealthy during the lengthy crossing. From *Sejlskibe og Sømænd i forrige århundrede* (Sail Ships and Seamen in the Last Century) (Copenhagen: Chr. Erichsens Forlag, 1975), courtesy Norwegian Emigrant Museum

the decades after the Civil War. But before the mass emigration, in a founding phase lasting from 1825 to 1865, 77,873 Norwegians crossed the Atlantic to make a home for themselves in America. More than half, or 39,359, left in the decade 1856–65. It was to a great extent a rural-to-rural migration or in some instances rural-to-urban. Only in the 1850s did a substantial urban-to-urban movement arise, with a sudden surge of emigration overseas from some of Norway's cities, especially from the capital city of Christiania (Oslo). Among those who left were many craftsmen and artisans; frequently adult men who emigrated had special occupational skills. Chicago became a major destination. But only during the latter years of the 1850s did Norwegians begin settling in Chicago in large numbers. An established immigrant community then functioned like a magnet. In 1860 Norwegian-born Chicagoans numbered 1,573, and by the close of the decade 6,825 were recorded. During the entire period under consideration, until the end of the Civil War, most people went to America in family units, making a permanent move to begin life over in a different part of the world.

The history of the early migration from eastern Norway must be placed in a broader national historical context. The narrative so far has mainly concentrated on the lives and departures of the central subjects from Lier and Tinn. The pioneer exodus from eastern Norway connected directly with the movement from southwestern Norway, as did migration from all other parts of the country—the beginning of a dramatic national experience.

Norwegian migration had a wavelike pattern—an ebb and flow of the crossing—as "America fever," as the urge to go to America was called already in 1837, moved like a dangerous disease that could not be contained from the southwestern coastal regions to fjord localities farther north and to the valleys of eastern Norway. The spread of information likely determined when emigration from specific districts occurred. "America letters" and guidebooks provided knowledge about America, a land that promised personal advancement and freedom. These assurances became a decisive factor for people who already were inclined to leave the homeland for a better future across the Atlantic.

A major characteristic of emigration was its uneven distribution and intensity within Norway. In spite of great local differences, by the end of the founding phase the whole country was represented. Most of the emigrants had, however, come from the inner fjord districts in West Norway and the mountain valleys in East Norway. Immigrants from these regions of Norway, as I state in *The Promise of America*, first shaped a Norwegian immigrant community and gave it "a content and direction that reflected the traditions, mores, and religious as well as secular values of their Norwegian home districts."

There existed constant encouragement to emigrate, pressure that was especially strongly felt in the regions with the highest rates of emigration. These regions experienced population growth that outstripped available resources and a lack of alternative employment outside the home district. But rather than employing a weighty term like "overpopulation" as a direct cause of emigration, instead one should view the increase in population simply as a heavy burden placed on local resources. Material resources were not the only reason people left the confining rural community. It is important to keep firmly in mind that the resolve to emigrate represented for the individual a personal decision. However, Vik in Sogn and Tinn in Upper Telemark, the first a fjord community and the second a mountain valley, may typify certain similarities—social, economic, and demographic—in regions that experienced emigration in the period before 1865.

The situation in Tinn has already been considered, but a contemporary observation and some closing analysis give added insight. In 1845 the provincial governor in Stavanger saw the emigration

from Tinn as being far from a flight but instead undertaken in hope
of achieving "a gentler existence." Between 1841 and 1845 each family emigrating from Tinn took along considerable resources. Recent
Norwegian research views the initial emigration as a stage in up-
ward mobility. Emigration from the lower social classes in peasant
society—cotters, tenants, and laborers—became noticeable only in
the 1850s. Prepaid tickets from earlier Tinn emigrants frequently
financed the journey. Such prepaid tickets played an important role
in enabling people to emigrate and opened the way west for Norwegians at all levels of society. By 1892, as recorded by some carriers,
more than 70 percent of one-way tickets from Norway on their lines
were purchased in the United States and sent to Norway. Norwegian
settlements throughout the nineteenth century stood ready to receive
newcomers.

Circumstances in the community of Vik located on the Sogne-
fjord had many similarities with Tinn. Vik became the major area of
emigration from Sogn. An agricultural system bound by tradition
and hampered by impractical strip farming (*Teigblanding*) was inca-
pable of expanding production to keep pace with the demand the
rapidly growing population created. There was regular emigration
from Vik beginning in 1841. After people learned about opportunities
in America, the floodgates opened—as I relate in my history of the
migration—and people sought their future in America. People from
Sogn also explored opportunities elsewhere in Norway, but America
eventually became almost the exclusive destination for those who
left their home community. Emigration became a safety valve that
reduced an acute strain on resources. The pressure to leave was felt
not only by the landless rural classes but also by independent farmers in constrained circumstances, who, as the provincial governor
reported in 1845, "have sold their property and afterward emigrated
to North America."[12]

Settlement

Historian Carlton C. Qualey emphasizes that Norwegian settlement must not be viewed as "a part of the process of emigration from Norway to the American shore and thence inland," but "as a separate process—an integral part of the westward movement of the American population." Norwegian immigrants did indeed join the westward movement of the American population. The founding of the Fox River settlement in LaSalle County, Illinois, in 1834 is of primary significance, as it became the initial destination for Norwegian immigrants and took on the role of a mother settlement. The Fox River settlement expanded and had several branches as newcomers took land in neighboring townships. Desirable lands in the vicinity of the Fox River settlements were eventually occupied. Reports of good lands to be had farther westward and northward reached those in the expanded Fox River settlement, and families and individuals migrated to regions out on the frontier, purchasing oxen and wagons for the move to new lands. Qualey assesses the Fox River settlement's importance in the spread of Norwegian homesteading: "One is tempted to regard the migration westward from New York to Illinois in 1834 as equal in importance to the voyage of the *Restauration*, for this small group migration was a pattern that was followed again and again as thousands of Norwegians pressed westward from one frontier to the next."

In the 1840s Wisconsin became the main region of Norwegian settlement, and the state remained the center of Norwegian American activity until the Civil War. In the summer of 1838 Ole Nattestad became the first Norwegian landowner in Wisconsin, moving from Illinois to the new location. His brother, Ansten Nattestad, was then in Norway.

As stated earlier, the Nattestad brothers had come to America via Gothenburg in early summer 1837. In Detroit, on their way west, they met Ole Rynning and the party he led on the bark *Ægir*, which

landed in New York on June 9. Like Rynning and party, the Natte-
stads made it to Detroit by way of Lake Erie. Ole and Ansten, instead
of continuing on to the Fox River settlement, joined the party to
lands selected under the influence of speculators in Beaver Creek in
Iroquois County, Illinois.

The Beaver Creek settlement became a colossal failure. Spring
rains and thaws in 1838 inundated the flat land, and a severe malaria
epidemic invaded the settlement. Most of the newcomers succumbed.
In the winter of 1837–38 Rynning wrote his greatly influential *True
Account of America* there; the volume was taken back to Norway,
as reported earlier, by Ansten Nattestad. Rynning died that fall and
was buried in an unmarked grave on the prairie. He was among the
many who perished.

Peter Testman, a tinner in the city of Stavanger, emigrated in the
spring of 1838, together with two of his brothers. They set up house in
the small and short-lived Norwegian Shelbyville settlement in Shelby
County, Missouri, on a site selected the year before by Cleng Peerson. Peter's experience in the pioneer community was not a happy
one, and in 1839 he returned to Norway empty-handed and disillu-
sioned. Testman wrote a small book in which he paints a gloomy
picture of his experience and of the New World—an antidote to the
books that were portraying an all-too-bright view of America and
thus raising expectations that could not be fulfilled. American streets
were not paved with gold. On the journey back home in the spring of
1839 Testman passed through the Fox River region and wrote about
the Beaver Creek settlement: "Here I met also some of the Norwegians who had emigrated by way of Bergen two years before and who
first settled farther south in Illinois at Beaver Creek, but who, after
student Rynning and many others died as a result of the unhealthful
climate, fled from their houses and lands after having lost nearly
everything they owned."

After the Beaver Creek settlement broke up Ole Nattestad first removed to the Fox River settlement and then to Wisconsin, where on July 1, 1838, he staked an eighty-acre claim in what became known as Jefferson Prairie in Rock County. He was joined by other new-comers as he recorded in his diary: "Toward the end of September, 1839, I received a group of people from my home community who as emigrants had followed my brother Ansten from Norway. Most of them settled on Jefferson Prairie, and in this manner this settlement in a comparatively short time got a large population."

The rising tide of Norwegian immigration manifested itself in the Territory of Wisconsin. Following approval of statehood by the territory's citizens, Wisconsin entered the Union on May 29, 1848, as the thirtieth state. Norwegian immigrants took up farming in exceptional numbers wherever they settled in the Upper Midwest—and did so in larger percentages than any other major immigrant group in the nineteenth century. By the 1870s the major areas of Norwegian settlement in Wisconsin had been demarcated, and they have in large part persisted until the present time. Individual settlements will be identified in later passages. Settlements in the southeastern and southern counties and some in the northeastern and north-central counties were established in the 1840s and 1850s, and the north-western and western counties were settled after migration into Iowa and Minnesota had begun. Hans Christian Heg, as a young man in Muskego, became a guide to new settlements; his efforts in that regard will be considered in the following chapter.

The US census of Wisconsin shows that Norwegian immigrants in 1850 made up 3 percent of the state's inhabitants, 9,467 people; in 1860 there were 29,557 Norwegian-born settlers, or 3.8 percent, and a decade later 59,619, or 5.6 percent of the population. If statistics were available, one might add to these figures the American-born Norwegians; Norwegians were the most numerous of the three

Scandinavian groups in Wisconsin, and among the foreign stock outnumbered only by the Germans.

Norwegians moved westward into northeastern Iowa in the late 1840s together with thousands of American settler colonists. Iowa shifted to statehood from territory in 1846. Direct from Norway, the immigrants could reach the state via the Mississippi River from New Orleans, or they could take the land route from Wisconsin and Illinois, joining the exodus from older settlements. Winneshiek County in northeastern Iowa became the largest Norwegian settlement area. Settlers from Dane and Racine Counties, Wisconsin, moved to Winneshiek County in 1849, and the following year twelve families from the same region founded the Washington Prairie settlement. Most of the immigrants were from Voss, Telemark, Sogn, and Valdres, and had first stayed some years in Wisconsin. Direct immigration from Norway to Iowa began as early as the summer of 1853, when a large group of immigrants arrived from Christiania (Oslo). On July 1, 1853, *Emigranten* reported the rapid growth of the town of Decorah. By 1860 there were 4,207 Norwegians in the county.

Norwegian pioneer settlers moved to the northern counties bordering Minnesota, forming settler colonies and becoming landowners, especially in Mitchell, Worth, and Winnebago, with a smaller group in Emmet. Pastor C. L. Clausen, an early Lutheran religious leader, was in 1853 instrumental in founding the village of St. Ansgar in Mitchell County, which became the nucleus for an extensive Norwegian settlement. The two settlements in Story County reveal how ruptures within the Lutheran church played a role in their founding. In 1855 a large group of immigrants from Sunnhordland on the west coast of Norway had arrived at the Fox River area and found that all land was taken there. Scouts sent to Story County brought the welcome news of large stretches of government land. The men acquired teams of oxen and made their wagons ready. Before leaving the Fox

River district, the colonists organized themselves as a Lutheran congregation and took the promising name Palestine. A total of 106 people traveled west in ox-drawn covered wagons—twenty-one families, five bachelors, and one widow. The colonists left on May 16, 1855, and arrived at their destination on June 7. The party formed the so-called southern settlement in Story County.

A party of Haugeans in the farm communities by the Fox River also sent agents to central Iowa and formed a colony farther north. Religious conviction lent strength but simultaneously separated the two colonies, even though they had the same local origin in Norway. The population census for Iowa in 1850 counts only 330 Norwegians; ten years later 8,048 Norwegians were recorded. By 1870, 25,251 Norwegians resided in Iowa, equal to 2.1 percent of the total state population.

In 1850 the celebrated Swedish author Fredrika Bremer made a strenuous and brief visit to the small city of St. Paul, capital of the territory of Minnesota. According to the census of 1850, there were only nine Norwegians in Minnesota; two of these were soldiers at Fort Snelling. After returning to Sweden Bremer in 1853 published *The Homes of the New World*, in 1855 made available to Norwegian and Danish readers in a Danish translation. In addition to Bremer's classic America book, several other emigrant guides were published in the early 1850s, both in Norway and in Denmark. Bremer's book became an influential and widely read work in all the Scandinavian countries, as it was in England and the United States. Bremer wrote: "What a glorious new Scandinavia might not Minnesota become! . . . The climate, the situation, the character of the scenery agrees with our people better than that of any other of the American States, and none of them appear to me to have a greater or a more beautiful future before them than Minnesota."

Bremer's vision and prophecy were to become a reality within the next twenty-five years. The early 1850s introduced the first period of settlement in Minnesota, which lasted until 1865. The large Goodhue County was opened to settlement the spring of 1852. The earliest settlement area was south of Goodhue County, however; beginning in 1851 parties of Norwegian settlers moved to western Houston and eastern Fillmore along the Iowa border. In southern Houston County the Norwegian Spring Grove settlement, founded in 1852, became a center in one of America's most densely populated Norwegian colonies. Carlton Qualey maintains the following about Spring Grove: "This settlement was one of the important distribution points for Norwegian settlement in the American Northwest, and there are hundreds of Norwegian Americans in western Minnesota and the Dakotas whose ancestors stopped for a time in Spring Grove Township before going on farther westward."

While immigrants had to make the long journey from Chicago or Milwaukee overland in oxcarts, immigration to Minnesota was limited. But in the spring of 1854 the railroad between Chicago and Rock Island on the east bank of the Mississippi was completed, inaugurating a new era of development for the Upper Mississippi Valley. Settlers could go by steamboat up the Mississippi to St. Paul or they could cross the river and proceed to their destination on foot or in wagons drawn by oxen procured at the river towns. No railroad was operated within Minnesota until 1862.

Minnesota gained statehood in 1858. From the 1860s on, population growth was strongly marked by people born outside America who migrated into the state. Most Norwegians at that time came to Minnesota via Quebec. Migration continued during the Civil War. Western expansion was given a powerful boost when the Homestead Act was passed in 1862. The main region of Norwegian settlement developed in the northern part of the so-called Homestead Act triangle between the Missouri and Mississippi Rivers, in an area where there was much government land. Great numbers of Norwegians, whether coming directly from Norway or from older settlements, were pulled along in the westward movement and chose to become pioneer farmers.

The number of Norwegians who made Minneapolis their home was not large in the early period of settlement, but it increased steadily. By the 1870s the infant metropolis near St. Anthony Falls, with its growing Norwegian population, institutions, and societies, gradually came to function like a Norwegian American capital and commercial center for the widespread Norwegian settlements throughout the Upper Midwest. Among the Norwegian immigrants were also many skilled laborers, professionals, and tradespeople who took up their old occupations in the New World, as seen in Chicago, and common laborers who lacked sufficient capital to start farming. Many moved to Minneapolis.

The total number of Norwegians in Minnesota rose from a handful in 1850 to 6,769 in 1857. The US census recorded 11,893 Norwegians in 1860, which in the following decade rose to 49,509.

By the eve of the Civil War, as Blegen describes it, "the Norwegian immigration, which had begun not forty years before with a handful of immigrants settling on the New York frontier, had swept westward to the spacious valley of the Mississippi and was striking deep roots in several states beyond the river." Norwegians "figured in the peopling and development of America's inland empire . . . and they identified themselves with the Northwest." In 1860 in the states of the Upper Midwest—Illinois, Wisconsin, Iowa, and Minnesota—were about fifty-five thousand people of Norwegian birth or ancestry. About 68 percent of them had been born in Norway. There were perhaps a thousand Norwegians elsewhere in America.

The Civil War was a watershed experience for the Norwegian immigrant community, marking a decisive phase in the process of adjusting to their new homeland. The enormous conflict created a new sense of patriotism, a sense of having earned a legitimate place in America. Norwegian immigrants, newcomers, and settler colonists responded to the call for volunteers to an exceptional degree after the outbreak of hostilities. Not only Norwegians but immigrants of all nationalities volunteered or were drafted in numbers that more than equaled their percentage of the population—in part because more of them were in the age prescribed for military service. The Norwegian Fifteenth Wisconsin Regiment under the leadership of Colonel Hans Christian Heg became a symbol of the patriotism of Norwegian Americans.[13]

CHAPTER 2

ᨠᨠ

Life on the American Frontier

MUSKEGO

The Muskego settlement some twenty miles from Milwaukee is one of the most noteworthy of the Norwegian pioneer settlements. Muskego fostered Hans Christian Heg, and from there he became one of the first Norwegian Americans to gain military fame. Søren Bache relates in his diary for August 30, 1840, the arrival in Muskego of the Heg family, who landed in Milwaukee after making the long journey west from New York, and his and Johannes Johansen's meeting with Even Heg at their property at Wind Lake.

I heard the voices of Even Heg and Johansen outside and our hired man came running in to announce the arrival of Even Heg. I rushed out to meet him. The joy of seeing old friends in so distant a land can surely be appreciated by anyone. He had arrived in Milwaukee with his company this morning and was brought to our place by a Norwegian. Fortunately we were able to serve him a cup of tea and some fresh fish which our man had caught. After eating, we retired because he was weary from his day's walk. The house was so small that we had to take out the bedstead and make a pallet on the floor. But in spite of his weariness there was no sleep all night long because of

the ceaseless flow of questions and answers. Thus went the first night
of our reunion.

In his essay "Muskego," published in *Symra* in 1907, Hjalmar
Rued Holand describes in detail the founding of the Muskego settlement in 1839 by the emigrant party led by John Nelson Luraas
from Tinn and Hjartdal in Upper Telemark. A party of emigrants
from Stavanger joined the Luraas party in Gothenburg. The Stavanger party proceeded to the Fox River district in Illinois, the intended
destination, whereas the Telemarkians abandoned their initial plan.
As Holand describes it, after landing in Milwaukee they were met
by "Milwaukee's enterprising merchants," who were impressed by
"these strong hardworking newcomers." They would be splendid
people to build up Milwaukee's surrounding country. The merchants
formed a committee "to emphasize the advantages for the Norwegians of the Milwaukee's environs." They were in the strongest terms
warned by a land agent against moving on to Illinois, "where they
will only find barren land, where heavy storms raged, while the sun
burned off what they raised, and the malaria fever devoured people
like flies."

The land agent along with, to follow Holand's account, "a committee of city folk and immigrants" helped find a satisfactory place
for a colony. The nearest region where some large land areas were
not yet settled was near Lake Muskego in Waukesha County, southwest of Milwaukee. The Norwegian settlers were not aware of the
marshy and soggy landscape they were inspecting, as the marsh-
land had dried up during the summer heat and resembled large
grasslands. The immigrants from Tinn thought the land was beautiful and returned to Milwaukee, where all of them, as Holand has
it, procured a piece of land, happy to have found a home after their
long journey.

The Muskego settlement thus becomes an example of unwary immigrants being exploited by dishonest land agents, in this case supported by aggressive city leaders. The lack of knowledge of English was a serious handicap for the immigrants, as was their ignorance of American conditions. They were easy prey to fraudulent speculators. The land selected, as the county records for September 16, 1839, show, proved to be similar to that in the ill-fated Beaver Creek colony in Illinois. As in Beaver Creek, the land seemed dry in the fall but became swampy in the spring. Muskego was likewise to suffer from malaria and cholera epidemics during the first dozen years of its history. Nevertheless, the settlers stayed.

The arrival in 1840 of Even Heg and the party he led did much to build up the colony. By virtue of his character and his financial means, Heg became the colony's acknowledged leader. The new

The cabin of Søren Bache in Muskego, Wisconsin. Norwegian-American Historical Association

immigrants went directly to Muskego, but on the advice of correspondence from Søren Bache took lands in the expanded Muskego
colony in Racine County, southeast of Waukesha County. Even Heg's
immediate contact with Bache at Wind Lake was thus significant.
The lands on Wind Lake became Norway Township, Racine County.
Heg purchased a large tract of land and sold much of it again to later
comers on liberal terms. On September 2, Bache describes in his diary
how he and Johansen, assisted by Heg and companions, decided to
build a house and make use of a mound out on a fine plot of ground
with good drainage "in all directions. The job was soon completed."
The mound, as Bache explains, "proved to be an Indian grave." He
justified building a dwelling there by claiming that "By now these
burial customs have doubtless been discarded." Svein Nilsson shared
the following description in *Billed-Magazin* (Picture Magazine), on
November 29, 1868: "An Indian mound was excavated, the walls
lined with boards, and the place fixed up as store, kitchen, and living
room. . . . The Indian mound became, in many respects, the heart of
the settlement. Here was the seat of culture and learning, the center of
pomp and luxury, the stronghold of finance." Bache continued to be
one of the leaders in the settlement and attracted more immigrants
by his letters. The name Muskego was retained after most of the settlers moved away from the lowlands originally selected and settled
in Norway Township and adjoining townships in Racine County.

   In the early fall of 1842 Jakob Olsen Einong (Einung) and his
diminished family reached the Old Muskego Norwegian settlement
following the tragic loss of wife Anne and daughter Suzanne, both of
whom died during the extended Atlantic crossing. Of the ten members of the Einung family who had left Norway in the summer of
1842, now, months later, only eight remained. There were four girls:
Anne, twenty-two, who was Suzanne's twin and, as *Telesoga* has it,
"a rather frail, sickly young woman"; Aslaug, seventeen; Gunild,

who would later marry Hans Christian, ten; and Gro (Gurine), seven. There were three boys: Ole, fifteen; Jon (later John), thirteen; and Osten (later Austin), five.

After their arrival in Muskego, Jakob purchased forty acres of land for each of his children and must have believed he had secured their future in the New Land. He might also have felt some self-recrimination about his wife's and daughter's deaths. However, he did not have many months to experience either contentment or guilt. In the fall of 1843 an epidemic of cholera broke out in the community, and Jacob succumbed to the disease. Deaths in the Muskego community were numerous that winter. Tragic tales of sudden death, and the orphans left behind, relate the tribulations that faced settler colonists on the American frontier. Waves of epidemic illness struck the Muskego community and brought widespread grief.

The remaining Einong children were considered orphans. *Telesoga* observed: "These youngsters must have felt themselves deserted by parents who had taken them to this new land which had promised so much, but, so far, had given them only painful loss. One can only guess how fervently they must have longed for their old, familiar life in Norway."

Aslaug, as the second-oldest in the family, assumed much of the responsibility for her younger siblings. People stepped in to help each other. Two newly arrived bachelors, John Molee and Hans Tveito, took it upon themselves to remove and bury the bodies of the dead, sparing men with families from assuming this dangerous role. Relationships quickly blossomed between John and Anne and between Hans and Aslaug. By Eastertime 1844, the two couples were married in a double ceremony. The Molee couple lived in a two-story log house John had built. They had five children, all born in Muskego.

There were not only romantic but practical reasons for Aslaug and Hans Tveito's union, since, as the saying goes, a man needs a wife to prosper on a farm. But Hans also provided the help and care of an older and strong man to the parentless Einong family. The Tveitos settled into the Muskego community, where they helped care for Aslaug's younger siblings while starting their own family. Hans had a reputation as a man of strength and moral courage. Although ten years his junior, "Aslaug was known throughout her life as a woman who made hard-headed practical decision[s]."[1]

A MOTHER COLONY

Proximity to Milwaukee partly explains why Muskego became such a noteworthy Norwegian settlement. In the 1840s Milwaukee functioned as an important gateway for immigrants to Wisconsin and areas farther west. Muskego became a mother colony and a distribution point for the multitude of arriving Norwegian immigrants. In 1843 Johan R. Reiersen, editor of the reform newspaper *Christianssandsposten*, in which he spoke enthusiastically about America and encouraged emigration, set out for America to study conditions there as the representative of some would-be emigrants. Muskego was one of the settlements Reiersen visited. Returning to Norway in 1844, he published *Veiviser for Norske Emigranter til De Forenede Nordamerikanske Stater og Texas* (Pathfinder for Norwegian Emigrants to the United States and Texas). Reiersen recounted in *Pathfinder* his critical opinion of Muskego and Wind Lake:

> The whole region is flat, with many marshes. The tillable elevations—rising only slightly above the level of the marshes—consist of glades between forests of white oak and the soil is a thin layer of mould over a stratum of clay. Immigrants from Voss, Telemarken, Numedal and elsewhere, have settled in this region and have begun to till the land, but the crops are not yet sufficient to supply the needs of the settlers. . . . It is rather expensive, furthermore, to clear the land, and

the soil is less fertile than is usual elsewhere. About two hundred families have purchased land, chiefly in small lots of forty acres each; only a few have larger tracts and as many own no land at all. The population in 1843 was estimated at between fifteen hundred and two thousand, but of these a large number planned to push on into the interior in the spring.

Muskego never became very large; people in general, like Reiersen, had an unfavorable opinion of it. Still, the original settlement continued to grow, until the great cholera epidemics in 1849, 1850, and 1852. During these years every household experienced deaths and suffered greatly. The settlers moved away, and the old colony was almost abandoned. The original Muskego settlement declined in the 1850s from thirty-six families to only seven. Carlton Qualey nevertheless underscores that in 1850 the extended settlement, including Muskego Township in Waukesha County and the townships of Norway, Raymond, Rochester, Waterford, and Dover in Racine County, consisted of 171 families and 912 persons. The Racine settlement, mainly Waterford and Dover townships, experienced some growth. But during the decade of the 1850s, according to census figures, the entire settlement decreased to 135 families and 728 persons. The population thereafter remained fairly constant, the natural growth keeping ahead of the westward movement. By the sixties, Muskego was no longer the important transit route that it had been in the previous two decades.

Immigrating at the age of eleven, Hans Christian passed the remaining years of his youth in this pioneer frontier community. In the words of people who knew him, cited by several historians, he soon earned the reputation of being "a wide-awake and gifted boy." He naturally retained a fluent command of the language of his childhood, living as he did in a community where Norwegian was generally

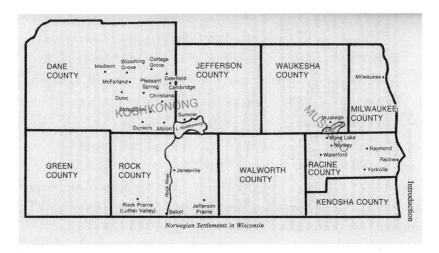

Norwegian Settlements in Wisconsin

Norwegian settlements in Wisconsin. Note the expanded Muskego settlement. From C. A. Clausen, *A Chronicle of Immigrant Life*, courtesy Norwegian-American Historical Association

spoken. He still took great pains to learn to use English and appears to have done so with ease. Indeed, his Civil War letters were written in the language of his adopted country. Growing up, there were new duties and adjustments. The death of his mother, Siri (Sigrid) Olsdatter Heg, on October 13, 1842, when she was only forty-three years old, was a tragic loss for the Heg family. Hans Christian would turn thirteen in December of that year; as the oldest of his siblings, he must have found that his mother's passing placed new burdens on his young shoulders. Being a teenager further exacted its own adult commitments and responsibilities.

In the 1840s Muskego became, as Carlton Qualey describes it, a depot where the hundreds of immigrants arriving from Milwaukee stopped for a time until they could go on to lands recommended by the Muskego settlers. Even Heg won fame as a sagacious adviser to the hundreds of immigrants who stopped temporarily at Muskego on their way west. Even Heg, Søren Bache, and Johannes Johansen gave much aid to the less fortunate immigrants whose funds had been exhausted by the expenses of the long journey. Hans Christian assisted his father and the other men as they sustained the impoverished new arrivals. These men also purchased land in considerable amounts and divided the parcels into small lots to resell. Heg's purchase of a large tract of land at Wind Lake is noted earlier.

Some of the impoverished Norwegians who came to the Muskego settlement prospered as farmers in the course of a decade or two. Blegen gives as an example the experience of Mons K. Aadland from Samnanger municipality, some twelve miles east of the city of Bergen, who in 1840 went north from the Beaver Creek settlement, the last person to do so, with three dollars and a few head of cattle. He settled east of what became Muskego and opened up the prairie and wooded groves to settlement. Eighteen years later he was worth $40,000 and had eight hundred acres of land and much valuable farm equipment.

Most of those who acquired land by Lake Muskego did not fare as well, and many moved away from the settlement. Bache describes the arrivals in 1843, a heavy immigrant year, and the dire conditions in the Muskego settlement. One entry in his diary provides insight into the ominous circumstances and outlook that confronted the immigrants even prior to the disastrous epidemics in the late 1840s and early 1850s. According to Bache, more than seventy people died from the epidemic during the fall of 1843, Jakob Einong among them. One reason for these deaths, Bache points out, was the fact that after the immigrants landed in Milwaukee they came to the settlement wagonload after wagonload, most of them too poverty-stricken to go farther. "They had nothing to live on," Bache continues, "and the older settlers had to take care of them, with the result that fifteen to twenty people were frequently crowded into a house. One after the other was taken ill." Another contributing factor was the lack of an adequate number of wells, and as a consequence in most houses there was nothing to drink but brown marsh water. Bache's conclusion: "While they were in this miserable state, they wrote letters home which were full of venom as their hearts were full of hatred for this place."

As people sought a life away from the homeland, the anticipated better future for themselves and their progeny persuaded them to emigrate. One may well ask how many immigrants later regretted their decision. No doubt there were also an untold number of success stories. The name Muskego came to have a special ring in the ears of new arrivals passing through the colony and becoming landowners farther west. The Muskego Manifesto, a document written by Johannes Johansen and dated January 6, 1845, might be viewed as the most dramatic defense of the immigrants' new home. The Muskego settlers were indignant over the excessive anti-emigration propaganda as well as the misinterpretation of American conditions that circulated in the homeland. Inserted in the major Oslo newspaper *Morgenbladet* on April 1, the manifesto was in the form of an open letter signed by eighty men. Even Heg was one of the leading signers, a fact that must have impressed young Hans Heg. They acknowledged difficulties, "caused by many kinds of illnesses and by lack of the most essential necessities of life." These could, the document states, be overcome and future prospects were bright. A section of the manifesto reads: "We harbor no hopes of acquiring wealth, but we live under a liberal government in a fertile land, where freedom and equality prevail in religious as well as civil affairs, and without any special permission we can enter almost any profession and make an honest living; this we consider to be more wonderful than riches, for by diligence and industry we can look forward to an adequate income, *and we thus have no reason to regret our decision to move here.*"

The Distribution-Preemption Act of 1841 made it easier to acquire land. On July 1, 1838, Ole Nattestad, the first Norwegian settler in Wisconsin, staked out an eighty-acre claim in what became Jefferson

Prairie, Rock County, Wisconsin. The extended Jefferson Prairie settlement by 1850 included 407 individuals, almost all making a living as farmers. Most of the company headed by Ansten Nattestad in 1839 settled there, but as Nattestad noted, "Some of them went to Rock Prairie, west of Beloit, and took land there." The Rock Prairie settlement, thus founded in 1839, is often called the Luther Valley settlement, after the Lutheran congregation that was established in 1844. The settlement, with a branch into Iowa, had by 1850 reached a total of 180 families and included 942 people. Muskego settlers regularly accompanied parties of newly arrived immigrants to settlements in the interior of Wisconsin; as a consequence Hans Christian made many trips to the Jefferson, Rock, and Koshkonong prairie settlements, piloting together with his father the newcomers looking for land in Wisconsin. "Such experience," Theodore C. Blegen states, "was not formal education, but must have played its part in widening the mental horizons of a keenly observant boy."

The Wisconsin Blue Book, 1933, assesses Hans Christian's experience guiding immigrants to Norwegian colonies: "In this way young Heg as he grew to manhood obtained a personal acquaintance with those fellow-countrymen who keep coming to Wisconsin in ever-increasing numbers." He also saw such significant historical milestones as the beginning of the first American newspaper printed in Norwegian and the first Wisconsin Norwegian Lutheran church, both to be fully narrated later. "Hans Heg," *The Wisconsin Blue Book* insists, "was a charter member of the new Scandinavian-American civilization which was growing up in Wisconsin prior to the Civil War."

In Dane County, "in the heart of Wisconsin, on the prairies which border the capital, Madison," Reiersen wrote after his visit in 1843, "a large number of the most recent Norwegian immigrants have formed several small settlements within a circuit of ten to twelve miles." Koshkonong, established in 1840 in eastern Dane County and western Jefferson County by settlers from Fox River and Jefferson

Prairie, was conceivably the most important, certainly the most prosperous, of the early Wisconsin settlements. The settlement grew large
by beautiful Lake Koshkonong and received its name from the lake,
Norwegianized as Kaskeland. There was considerable migration in
1843: "Most of the newcomers were from Muskego. Others had emigrated from Norway that same year, and after a temporary stay in
Milwaukee or Muskego, had continued on to Koshkonong." The growing immigration of the 1840s increasingly sent families directly from
Norway to the Koshkonong area. At the close of the forties there were
543 Norwegian families with a total of 2,670 residents in the townships included in the Koshkonong settlement. Increased immigration expanded the settlement's population in the succeeding decades.
By 1860 it numbered 3,699 persons in 633 families.

The fame of Koshkonong spread far and wide among Norwegian
immigrants in the United States and was made known across the
Atlantic in books, pamphlets, and letters. Articles in *Billed-Magazin*—
published weekly in Madison, October 3, 1868, to September 17, 1870,
and edited by Svein Nilsson, an immigrant from Namdalen, Norway—
are a major source on early Norwegian settlement in Wisconsin.
These articles made Nilsson "the father of Norwegian American historical writing." In *Billed-Magazin*, on February 5, 1870, Nilsson
affirms: "The whole area commonly referred to as Koshkonong was
settled and put under cultivation in a remarkably short period of
time, and the Norwegians took the lead, ahead of any other nationality. It seems as if here our countrymen first found the America of
which they had heard such wonderful stories in the homeland."

A family coming from Norway would usually stop for a while in an
older settlement before heading for regions farther west, and then
frequently on the advice of earlier immigrants who had left the older
area. As Norwegian immigrants streamed into Wisconsin, Muskego
was by the late forties no longer dominant as a point of dispersion,

preempted by Koshkonong, Rock Prairie, and Norwegian colonies farther west. The Koshkonong settlement became a leading mother colony to numerous settlements in Wisconsin and in other parts of the Middle West.[2]

EVEN HEG'S BARN AND THE MUSKEGO CHURCH

In *Billed-Magazin* for November 29, 1868, Svein Nilsson expands on how Even Heg offered the immigrants a helping hand. The large, home-sawed, oak-frame barn Heg erected on the family farm in the Town of Norway, Racine County, in 1843 is in this regard of special interest. It became famous throughout the Northwest because, as Nilsson describes the situation, many emigrants who came by way of Milwaukee could rest there after their strenuous ocean voyage before moving farther west. The small log cabins the settlers lived in had only one room, which served as kitchen, living room, and bedroom. There was thus little or no space to house strangers. Nilsson concludes: "A somewhat larger building, even though a barn, was viewed as a curiosity; and hundreds, if not thousands, of our countrymen—now scattered over the state—found lodging and hospitality here while on route to their new homesteads."

The Heg barn was not merely a haven for immigrants passing through; it was a social and religious center for the Muskego community. During the cholera epidemic of the late forties that desolated the colony, the barn also served as a hospital. Before a church was built in the community, lay services were held in the barn. Even Heg himself regularly preached, as did Bache, among others.

Many of the religious circumstances among Norwegians in America had their origin in Muskego. The arrival in 1843 of the pioneer pastor Claus L. Clausen—mentioned earlier as the founder of the St. Ansgar settlement in Iowa—is in this regard of great significance. Clausen was born on the island of Ærø in Denmark in 1820, the son

Even Heg erected a large home-sawed, oak-frame barn on the family farm in the Town of Norway, Racine County, Wisconsin, in 1843. Many Norwegian immigrants found lodging there before moving farther west. Norwegian-American Historical Association

of a merchant. He had spent time in Norway looking into missionary possibilities in South Africa. There he met the Haugean Tollef Bache, who instead encouraged him to go to Muskego as a teacher, serving children whose needs Bache, through his son Søren, was quite familiar with. Clausen took his advice and in 1843 joined a party of Norwegian immigrants headed for Muskego, arriving on August 3 along with his wife, Martha Rasmussen.

Clausen soon realized there was a greater need for a pastor and "became the first shepherd for the two hundred souls in the congregation" he organized on December 14 that same year. Despite strong sympathy for the Haugean pietism in the Muskego settlement, the first Norwegian Lutheran congregation in America came out of the high-church arrangement of the Church of Norway. C. L. Clausen approved of its traditional ecclesiastical vestments and liturgy. On

March 15, 1849, Clausen wrote in *Nordlyset* as a defender of the faith against "the sects which have gained proselytes." Clausen had studied theology but had never been ordained. A petition—signed by about seventy settlers looking for a spiritual leader—was sent to the German Lutheran pastor L. F. E. Krause to ordain "the well-known Danish evangelical Lutheran school teacher, Claus Lauritzen Clausen"; Pastor Krause received the proposal favorably and on October 18, 1843, conducted an ordination at the German settlement in Washington County, eighteen miles northwest of Milwaukee. Both Bache and Even Heg attended as witnesses at Clausen's examination—Krause, the examiner, using the German language since he knew neither English nor Norwegian. Pastor Clausen, as an ordained minister, held Sunday school classes in the barn, administered the sacred rites among the settlers, and at Easter 1844 conducted the first Norwegian Lutheran confirmation in America. That same year, as an

The Reverend Claus L. Clausen served the Muskego congregation he organized in December 1843 until 1846. Vesterheim Norwegian-American Museum

example of the broad use of Even Heg's "home-sawed, oak-frame barn," a double wedding was celebrated there.

Pastor Clausen served the congregation at Muskego until 1846, when he accepted a call from settlers in the Rock Prairie—or Luther Valley—settlement. At a meeting on December 23, 1843, eight trustees of the Muskego congregation considered whether the congregation should buy a forty-acre piece of land. Even Heg had promised he would sell off his property by Wind Lake at cost; the land had already been used as a burial ground. At the meeting no final decision was made. But on this parcel the first Norwegian Lutheran church in America was built. Even Heg, to quote Blegen, "in fact, donated the ground on which this historic edifice was erected." Gifts from Norway, including four hundred dollars from Tollef Bache, aided the Muskego settlers in putting up the church building.

On March 12, 1845, Bache noted in his diary that in the afternoon he, Johansen, and Heg had inspected the church, which then was almost completed. It was built of oak logs hewed on both sides, six inches thick, and matched after the Norwegian fashion of building houses. Bache described the interior of the church as attractive and noted that it was beautifully located on a hill in the heart of the Norwegian settlement. From the hill, as Bache notes, there was an excellent view in every direction for a distance of six to ten miles. Through the lowland toward the east, consisting primarily of unproductive marshes, there flowed a winding little stream out of Wind Lake to the north. Beyond the moors, as recorded by Bache, the land rose gently with occasional farmhouses on the hillside; he concluded that the scenery was indeed very beautiful and would be still more so in the full bloom of summer.

The Muskego Church was dedicated the following day, March 13. Søren Bache shares a lengthy account of the event, at times with critical comments The notable guests in attendance included Gustaf

Elias Unonius, educated at Uppsala University. In 1841 he emigrated to America and is best known as the founder of the New Upsala (Nya Uppsala) settlement by Pine Lake, located near what is now the town of Merton, Wisconsin—the first Swedish colony in the state. In 1845, after studying theology at the Nashotah Episcopal Seminary by Pine Lake, he was ordained as an Episcopal minister. Also present was the Middle West's prominent Episcopal leader and a founder of the Episcopal seminary James Lloyd Breck. J. W. C. Dietrichson, described as "an aristocratic, imperious, high-church diviner, of a military family," made his presence known. He immigrated at the age of twenty-nine in May 1844 as the first Norwegian Lutheran pastor in America ordained by a Norwegian bishop. He had great influence on and also

Den Förste Norsk Lutherske Kirke i Amerika 1843 - 69.
Muskego Kirken, Racine Co., Wis.

The Old Muskego Church was the first Norwegian Lutheran Church built in America, dedicated March 13, 1845. Norwegian-American Historical Association

a stormy career in the life of the immigrant church until returning to Norway in 1850.

In his diary account of the dedication, Bache—likely affected by his own Haugean convictions—is especially critical of Dietrichson and Clausen. In the sermon, delivered from the entry of the chancel, Dietrichson to Bache's dismay tried to inspire remorse in the hearts of the people for having left Norway, their dear native land. Dietrichson pictured "the idyllic life the immigrants had had among the mountains of Norway, where only one religion dominated the whole land." They had instead landed in an "American wilderness where many forsake the faith of their fathers and join erring sects." "It must be said," Bache concludes, "that the sermon as a whole was mixed with too much nonsense."

Pastor Clausen delivered his opening sermon in the new church from the pulpit over the altar. Bache is most critical of the message, more so than others like Even Heg. Indeed, Colonel Hans Christian Heg, as will be covered later, even recruited Clausen as the best qualified to serve as army chaplain for the Fifteenth Wisconsin. Bache depicts how Clausen dwelt at length on baptism "as the door which gives admittance to the communion of saints," and thereafter discussed the Lord's Supper. Clausen as his final point stresses the ministerial calling, "concluding by forbidding anyone but a Lutheran pastor to set foot in the place where he then stood." Bache, with his strong Haugean belief in lay preaching, observes that it was "a dictum that may not be so easy to enforce."[3]

RELIGIOUS CONTROVERSY

Among the number of "firsts" in Norwegian American history Muskego can boast were, according to Clarence Clausen in A Chronicle of Old Muskego, not only the first Norwegian church, mentioned above, but also that in the settlement "there was unleashed the first fury of those disputes which rent Norwegian-American Lutheranism through following generations." Clausen explains, "The settlement earned its distinction largely because of the outstanding leadership of a few men who lived there during the 1840s—men like Even Heg, Johansen, Pastor C. L. Clausen, Pastor J. W. C. Dietrichson and Bache himself, who all appear in the diary" of Søren Bache.

Religious strife occurred even during the construction of the church the fall of 1844, revealing the sensitivity of the most ardent Norwegian Haugeans to what were perceived as high-church ecclesiastics. Pastor Clausen's mandate that anyone wishing to receive communion should appear before the pastor a day in advance of receiving the sacrament aroused strong feelings and opposition; parishioners did not accept the explanation that the intention was not to exact a confession but simply an opportunity for the pastor to talk about the significance of gathering at God's table. Many, including Even Heg and Bache, instead regarded the mandate as a papistic yoke on their conscience and resigned from the congregation. The departed parishioners rejoined the congregation, but their resignation delayed completion of the church.

Many lay preachers early on voiced Haugeanism among the immigrants, thousands of whom were influenced by the Haugean movement. Church historian J. Magnus Rhone maintains: "In the bitter struggle between the clergy and Hauge . . . [the early immigrants] generally sided with Haugeanism against the State Church." Even so, these lay preachers, for the most part spreading antagonism against the established church of the homeland, met the settlers' first religious needs. Blegen sees the great zeal of the laymen leaders as testimony "to the power of the Haugean ferment and the fervency of religious feeling among the pioneers."

The evangelist Elling Eielsen (Sundve), a pietistic, anticlerical Haugean lay preacher, in his actions clearly towered far above the other revivalists. He was born in Voss, Norway, in 1804, the year of Hans Nielsen Hauge's final arrest and imprisonment for violating the ordinance against lay preaching. Like Hauge, Eielsen crisscrossed his homeland and even visited other Nordic countries as a zealous preacher. In 1839 Eielsen emigrated, arriving in the fall of that year in the Fox River settlement; he spent fully as much time in Muskego as in Fox River. Historian Rhone argues that there was a very noticeable difference between the two settlements in the attitude toward Elling Eielsen, even though both were Haugean, and traces the difference to the religious conditions in the homeland at the time of emigration. The settlers in Fox River were recruited chiefly from Stavanger and Rogaland, a district that had experienced religious persecution, while this was not true for the settlers from Numedal and Telemark who had settled in Muskego. The latter preferred a more positive church arrangement, while they rejected what they interpreted as high-church practices. The Haugeans in Muskego, led by Heg, Bache, and Johansen, dissociated themselves from Eielsen's fiery sermons. His derisive attacks on the Lutheran clergy produced only disgust in Muskego, whereas his assaults on the clerics were a source of strength and influence in the Fox River settlement.

Eielsen deserves great credit for establishing a low-church organization within the Lutheran free-church movement among Norwegians in America. In 1842 he built a combined dwelling and meetinghouse southwest of the village of Norway at Fox River, LaSalle County, Illinois. A sign wishing everyone "*Velkommen til Norway*" declares Norway, Illinois, "the first permanent Norwegian settlement in America." Following low-church practice, he termed it a *forsamlingshus*, an assembly house, not a church. Eielsen recognized the immigrants' attachment to organized church life and to Lutheran sacraments. Thus in 1843, at the wish of his followers, he let himself be ordained by a German Lutheran pastor. He thereafter functioned as a traveling missionary pastor, rather than as a lay preacher, in spreading his message. He had followers in almost every older, larger settlement, and especially his younger adherents made him see the importance of uniting his scattered flock in a church body. At a meeting in the pioneer Norwegian settlement Jefferson Prairie, Rock County, Wisconsin, on April 14 and 15, 1846, an assembly of his widely dispersed believers formulated a constitution and established a Lutheran low-church organization known as the Evangelical Lutheran Church in America. It became known as Elling Eielsen's Synod, or just Eielsen's Synod, and the members as Ellingians. Eielsen clung to it until his death at the age of seventy-five in 1883.

J. W. C. Dietrichson arrived in America on July 9, 1844, nearly thirty years old. The idea of coming to America was, as for Clausen, first awakened by an interest in missionary work in non-Christian societies, a notion that gained ground in Norway in the 1840s. Dietrichson was present at the Norwegian Missionary Society national convention in 1843. To minister to emigrated compatriots was a different calling, but they too needed religious guidance. In his brief publication *Reise blandt de norske Emigranter* (Journey among Norwegian Emigrants) he considers his mission in America: "To get information about the religious needs of the emigrated Norwegians, and to attempt to institute church order among them."

The extremely high-church Dietrichson clashed with the extremely low-churchly ideas of Eielsen, as Rhone states, and Dietrichson goes to great lengths in his publication to question the legitimacy of Eielsen's ordination and claimed that he *"ukaldet har trængt sig ind i Præsteembedet"* (uncalled has forced his way into the clerical office). Dietrichson also evaluates Clausen's entry into the ministry and concludes that he is *"en vakker Herrens Tjener"* (a commendable servant

The Reverend J. W. C.
Dietrichson. Norwegian-
American Historical
Association

of the Lord). Clausen thus fell in line with Dietrichson. Additionally, Clausen, as noted earlier, had a strong sympathy for Haugean pietism and in his beliefs placed himself between two Lutheran extremes. He was therefore accepted and well qualified for his work in the strongly Haugean Muskego settlement.

Dietrichson first came to the Muskego settlement in early August, where he conferred with Clausen, and set out very soon for Koshkonong, where he made his headquarters. In describing the five separate Norwegian settlements in Koshkonong Prairie, Rhone again makes his point of the impact of local differences in the Norwegian homeland. Most of the settlers at that time hailed from Telemark, Numedal, Voss, and Sogndal. It is a fact worth noting, Rhone insists, in view of the distinction already drawn above between these and the early immigrants from Stavanger and Rogaland in the Fox River settlement.

Koshkonong was still an unchurched settlement with a limited population, which, as outlined earlier, would increase rapidly in the 1840s. In his *Reise blandt de norske Emigranter*, Dietrichson relates his arrival and successive events in founding congregations, frequently in critical terms. In Koshkonong he made his dwelling in a small cabin that belonged to the first Norwegian settlers (he writes, "*jeg slog min Bolig opp*"). In addition to his travel narrative, there are Dietrichson's church records in the *Koshkonong Parish Journal* (*Kirkebog for Den Norsk Lutherske Menighed paa Koshkonongs Prairier*). Together the two sources provide a detailed record of Dietrichson's life and work in America, accessible to all in English translation, published by the Norwegian-American Historical Association in 1973.

In the lead entry in the parish journal, Dietrichson records his first three divine services in Koshkonong, August 30 and September 1 and 2, 1844. The first two were held in a barn, and for the third, as Dietrichson relates, "I conducted the service and administered the Lord's Supper out of doors under an oak tree on the farm of Knud Aslaksen Juve, in the western part of the settlement." The spot became a memorial to the pioneer church. Modern readers might benefit from reflecting on the difficult circumstances under which organized religious life was instituted. In all sermons Dietrichson reminded the parishioners of "their obligation to hold fast to the true saving doctrine of the church of our fatherland and its edifying ritual." A list of four conditions for membership was presented to the congregations he served, including these two: "Do you desire to belong to the Norwegian congregation here? To that end, are you willing to submit to the church order which the Church of Norway prescribes?" Doing so would ensure on American soil an unbroken continuity of the ritual and history of the Church of Norway.

Having decided upon his course of action, Dietrichson pursued his mission with great zeal and energy. On October 10, 1844, based on his points for membership he organized into a congregation forty families in the eastern part of the Koshkonong settlement in the town of Christiana—a misspelling of the name of the Norwegian capital Christiania—and three days later he organized thirty families into a congregation in the western part of the settlement in Pleasant Spring. He dedicated the West Church on December 19 of the same year with a sermon that seemed to denounce the emigrants for leaving "a Christian and lovable land," where "the Lord had let you be born, educated, nourished and developed both spiritually and materially." He shared this mindset with the Norwegian State Church clergy. Dietrichson pursued organizing activities in other settlements in Wisconsin and Illinois. While Clausen was still pastor at Muskego, he and Dietrichson organized a number of other congregations, attached either to Muskego or to Koshkonong until they became independent.

In March 1845 the two congregations Dietrichson founded issued a call for him to serve as their pastor for five years. Dietrichson felt a need to return to Norway to seek aid and persuade suitable pastoral candidates to carry on the work in America. He departed that spring. Clausen served as pastor in his place and kept the church journal. The homeland never took the initiative to attend to the immigrants' spiritual and physical needs. Aid from Norway was forthcoming, but in the form of private donations, as with Tollef Bache. Because the hierarchy in the mother church showed little concern for the emigrants, the university-trained pastors who sought to work in the Norwegian colonies acted on their own. Dietrichson's fervent missionary activity did, however, bring over to America talented young Norwegian theologians. Before returning to Koshkonong the summer of 1846, he married Charlotte Josine Omsen Muller, a woman of proper social aristocratic status.

A parsonage was built conveniently halfway between the two congregations, replacing the small hut that had been Dietrichson's dwelling. It was not a desirable location, however, because, to quote the journal, "the parsonage is surrounded by the meanest people in the whole congregation." There were disagreements, strife, and disturbance, and as recorded, "the effect on the weak members has been that they have sided more or less with the manifest enemies of the church." The parsonage provided a rallying point for members who hated the pastor and church order. Dietrichson records many of these disturbing episodes and his own uncharitable and vengeful response. Søren Bache chronicles some of these regrettable incidents as well and deplores Dietrichson's "behavior among Norwegians in Wisconsin," concluding that "although he came here as a pastor of souls to lead people away from evil, the result has been quite otherwise."

Organizing the individual Lutheran congregations into a church body was of course a natural next step. Although achieving unity was a major goal for Dietrichson, when he returned to Norway permanently in 1850 he had not succeeded. Arriving young university-trained pastors would carry the work forward. They responded to the lack of pastoral leadership among their countrymen in America. In 1848 H. A. Stub, descended from a family of pastors and bishops, arrived in Wisconsin to fill the Muskego parish left vacant the year before when Clausen accepted a call from the Luther Valley congregation. Stub was a man of tact and poise, and he and Even Heg became friends. A number of Norwegian theologians arrived in 1850–52; they were all among the founders of the church body that became known as the Norwegian Synod; among them were G. F. Dietrichson, who in 1851 took Clausen's place at Luther Valley when Clausen retired from active ministry for ten years due to poor health; N. O. Brandt, who joined the faculty at Luther College in Decorah, Iowa, in 1862, a year after the school was established; A. C. Preus—J. W. C. Dietrichson's brother-in-law—who took charge of organizing a synod; and H. A. Preus, who later became the chief and leader of the Norwegian Synod for a generation.

Before moving back to Norway, J. W. C. Dietrichson had in 1849 called a meeting at Koshkonong of delegates elected by the congregations. Clausen and Stub were not able to attend, but they cooperated with Dietrichson, who at the meeting read his sketch of a synodical constitution.

Work to organize a synod was taken up by A. C. Preus at a meeting of pastors and congregations at Luther Valley on January 4, 1851. Dietrichson's 1849 draft of the constitution was actually adopted together with an organizational form. The congregations met for renewed consultations at Muskego on February 1, 1852. Then the church established in 1851 was dissolved when the congregations adopted J. W. C. Dietrichson's Grundtvigian Constitution, which proclaimed some of the teachings of N. F. S. Grundtvig. The lay church and the university-trained ministers were both anti-Grundtvigians. H. A. Preus, a stringent anti-Grundtvigian, attacked a sentence in the document stating that the church's doctrine was "what is revealed through the Word of God in our baptismal covenant and in the Old and New Testament's canonical books." The objectionable words about "our baptismal covenant" were removed on a motion by H. A. Preus; everyone voted for it except Clausen, who declared that the original paragraph expressed his belief.

An acceptable church constitution was adopted at a meeting in East Koshkonong on February 3, 1853. On October 3–7 of that same year there was a meeting in Luther Valley of those who accepted the constitution, comprised of seven pastors and representatives from seventeen congregations. After four years of endeavor the work of organization was completed and the Norwegian Evangelical Lutheran Church of America, as the name is listed in the constitution, became a reality. It was later known as the Norwegian Synod, or simply the Synod. The new church body was an independent American institution, but it embraced the high-church ritual and principles of the Church of Norway, defended the ban against lay preaching, was dogmatic in its teaching, and asserted churchly authority in all questions of doctrine. The fact that the Synod pastors wore the ecclesiastical garments of the Church of Norway surely symbolized the broader transfer of religious convictions and traditions. The Synod was the largest gathering of Norwegian Lutherans in America, and a legacy of J. W. C. Dietrichson and his vision of how to preserve among the immigrants the Lutheran faith they brought with them from home.

The Muskego church had not sent delegates to the church conference in 1853, showing the persistent Haugean strength among Norwegian immigrants. In all Norwegian colonies there were adherents of lay activity and of Haugean pietism and religious intensity. H. A. Stub was unable to convince the Muskego congregation to join the Norwegian Synod because of opposition from powerful laymen. The resulting friction led Stub to resign from the Muskego pastorate in 1854.[4]

NORDLYSET—AND THE IMMIGRANT PRESS

A Norwegian-language press had its historic beginning in the New Land in 1847 when Even Heg launched the weekly *Nordlyset* (Northern Lights); strictly speaking, it was the first Norwegian-language journal in America. The Norwegian American press elicited throughout its long history debates about its own significance and impact in a maturing and steadily changing ethnic population. There can be no doubt that the immigrant press had a strong bridge-building function with the Norwegian homeland as well as a strong role in promoting Norsedom in America. The newspapers were a major force in maintaining a separate ethnic existence and bound together groups of Norwegians in all parts of the country, thereby giving meaning to the concept of a Norwegian America. Norwegian American journalism guided newcomers as well as their progeny in adjusting to the New Land. The individual journals were from early on political organs and encouraged Norwegian immigrants to enter public service. Knud Langeland, who attained great prominence in Norwegian American journalism, surmised that *Nordlyset* and its short-lived successor, the journal *Democraten* (The Democrat), were premature as political organs, however. Of peasant background, and in Norway not accustomed to subscribing to newspapers, Norwegian immigrants were likely not yet ready to sustain a separate Norwegian-language press.

The initial issue of *Nordlyset*, dated July 29, 1847, under the heading *Til vore Landsmænd* (To Our Countrymen), stated that its purpose was to enlighten Norwegian immigrants and provide those who lacked ability to read American newspapers "with an opportunity to acquire knowledge especially about this country's government." The articles thus emphasized American topics. Loyalty to the United States was evidenced in the same issue in a Norwegian translation of part of the Declaration of Independence and a cut of the American flag at the head of the editorial column. In addition to providing general information, history, and farming and religious news, *Nordlyset* promised "contributions from private individuals and everything else that may be suitable and useful for enlightenment and entertainment."

The paper announced that *Nordlyset* intended "to obtain the best Scandinavian newspapers regularly so that we can at all times report the most important accounts of these, so that we always can be informed about what is happening in our fatherland." In the age of sailing ships current news was not easily communicated. The newspapers from Norway arrived very irregularly or not at all, as *Democraten* complained on October 12, 1850. Only after the transatlantic telegraph cable crossed the Atlantic shortly after the Civil War had ended was regular news coverage from Norway, and Europe in general, possible. News from across the ocean, though dated, did make it to the immigrant journals earlier, however. In its February 24, 1848, issue *Nordlyset*'s editor thanked the Swedish-Norwegian consul general in New York, Adam Løvenskjold, for "a pack of *Morgenbladet* to the end of August 1847." The gift of the Norwegian newspaper enabled *Nordlyset* to publish in the same issue information about the 1847 election to the *Storting* (Grand Assembly), Norway's parliament. Such reporting would not occur on a regular basis, but there was indeed contact across the Atlantic.

It is significant that *Nordlyset* was launched by secular leaders rather than by the Lutheran clergy, which dominated religious life in the Norwegian immigrant community, including the pioneer press. In contrast, the newspaper *Emigranten* (The Emigrant) was closely associated with the Synod clergy. Even Heg and Søren Bache supplied most of the necessary funds and were joint publishers together with James D. Reymert. Bache relates in his diary that on June 27, 1847, he, Even Heg, Hans Christian Heg, and Reymert went to Milwaukee to fetch the printing press, paper, and other equipment. It was all installed in Even Heg's log cabin by Wind Lake in Norway, Racine County. The postal address was Norway, where Even Heg served as the postmaster. Even Heg was the leading figure in the Muskego community, and Hans Christian, who was eighteen years old when *Nordlyset* was established, assisted in the printing process. That the publishing office was in Heg's own home made it the political center of the community and consequently had great significance in Hans Christian Heg's political convictions. This subject will be more fully covered in the third chapter.

Young Reymert served as *Nordlyset*'s editor. Through *Nordlyset* he championed the "free-soil" movement. Blegen affirms that the most significant point in regard to the newspaper was that it became the

Norwegian organ of the Free Soil Party, founded in 1847–48 and gaining a following from the opponents of the spread of slavery to the western territories. The paper forecast, to cite Blegen, "the general course that the rank and file of Norwegians were to take in the stirring political controversy centering about the slavery issue in the next decade and a half." In 1848 the paper adopted as its motto the slogan of the Free Soil Party, "Free Land, Free Speech, Free Labor, and Free Men" (*Fri Jordbund, Fri Tale, Frit Arbeide og Frie Mænd*). *Nordlyset's* importance to Hans Heg was not simply that its publication office was in his home, but the fact that it took a definite stand on the main issue of the day and gave specific information about American politics.

Few later editors had Reymert's education and skill. Born in Farsund, Norway, in 1821, he spent five years in Scotland, his mother's native land, before coming to America in 1842. He there learned English and studied law. Reymert settled in Muskego in 1844. His work for *Nordlyset* became a successful springboard into American politics. From the start the immigrant press was a political tool for the newcomers.

Hans Christian Heg and Reymert harbored ill feelings against each other on political and perhaps also personal grounds. Heg strongly criticized Reymert, who had joined the Democratic Party, for his political convictions and the politicians he associated with. These feelings were expressed in rather chilling terms with the outbreak of the Civil War. Hans Heg and his brother, Ole Heg, then members of the Republican Party, attacked Reymert in a letter published in *Stavanger Amtstidende*, on July 16, 1861. The letter, as the newspaper explains, was obtained from a man in Lier who had lived a long time in America. The Hegs accuse Reymert of working "with all his might" (*for fulle Kræfter*) for the Democratic Party, which for a long time, Heg claims, had been controlled by the Southern states or in the interest of slaveholders.

In the fall of 1849 Langeland, as he himself relates, committed "the folly of buying the printing press from Heg and Reymert." He issued the last ten numbers of *Nordlyset* in the town of Racine, the final one dated May 18, 1850. When the next issue of the newspaper came out on June 8, the name had been changed to *Democraten*. Politically the newspaper moved toward the Democratic Party, but analogous to *Nordlyset*'s view, *Democraten* was strongly antislavery and advocated the Free Soil policy of free public lands. In the November 9, 1850, issue, Langeland accurately noted: "The slavery question is not between Democrats or Whigs, but between the North and South." The short-lived weekly's final number is dated October 29, 1851. Democratic candidate Reymert was elected to the Wisconsin state legislature, the first Norwegian to achieve such an honor.[5]

EMIGRANTEN—A PROMINENT PIONEER ORGAN

Emigranten (The Emigrant) was clearly the most important and best edited of the pioneer newspapers. The initial issue is dated January 23, 1852, at Inmansville, Rock County, Wisconsin, published by the Scandinavian Press Association (*Den Skandinaviske Presse-Forening*). Albert Barton points to the fact that the Norwegian American press was much more inclined to religious and theological controversy than the press in Norway. *Emigranten*'s founding represented the actions of prominent members of the Norwegian Synod clergy. The impetus came from the Synod's desire, on the initiative of C. L. Clausen, to publish a secular political newspaper in addition to its church periodical. *Emigranten* would give the Synod pastors a political voice. Despite *Emigranten*'s proposed status as a secular newspaper, Clausen was selected as its first editor. In *Emigranten*'s initial number, he declared that it would be "An Independent Democratic Newspaper" and chose the motto "Unity, Courage, Endurance" (*Enighed, Mod, Udholdenhed*). According to Barton, Charles M. Reese did most of the editorial work.

He, like Clausen, was a Dane by birth, but played a part in the development of the early Norwegian American press.

The first issue printed the newspaper's platform in English, making it clear that both Democratic and Whig opinions were represented in the press association. Under the heading "The Large American Political Parties: Whigs and Democrats" (*De store Amerikanske politiske Partier: Whigger og Democrater*), *Emigranten* endeavored to educate its readers about the principles of the two political entities as well as about America's naturalization laws and path to citizenship. Clausen strongly encouraged citizenship, because only then could Norwegians "contribute their part to the final development of this Great Nation." The newspaper had a clear Americanization message. Already in its fifth number, February 20, 1852, it printed in Norwegian translation the first of eighty chapters of a serialized history of the United States, from colonial times to the presidency of Andrew Jackson, titled "The United States or the American Republic's History" (*De Forenede Staters eller Den Amerikanske Republiks Historie*).

Emigranten, regardless of its intent to be a secular journal, gave much space to religious controversy. The pastors A. C. Preus, the Synod's president, and H. A. Preus, both serving on the board of the Scandinavian Press Association, engaged in bitter debates about church doctrine and polity. They were forceful supporters of the faith in the columns of *Emigranten*, defending what they judged to be "pure doctrine" and attacking what was thought to be "false teachings" by Lutheran clergy brethren. The association was dissolved in 1860, curtailing the Lutheran clergymen's role. "The clergy dominion (*Prestevældet*) has ended," the newspaper declared.

There were many signs that the Democratic Party was weakening among Norwegian voters in the Northwest. Albert Barton notes that the destruction by cyclone of *Emigranten*'s printing office and printing equipment in a stone building north of the Luther Valley church in a sense signaled definite change in political course. He writes that the Norwegians soon deserted the Democratic Party; "the cyclone of 1854 blew the Democracy out of the Norwegians" became a byword of the Norwegian settlements.

In 1854 *Emigranten*, in response to the views of association members, moved firmly into the newly organized Republican camp. The newspaper had earlier briefly accommodated with the Whig Party. But the division between proslavery and antislavery forces within the party, caused by the Kansas-Nebraska Act of 1854, broke up the Whig Party and became its death knell. The Kansas-Nebraska Act specified that settler colonists in the Kansas and Nebraska Territories would decide whether to be free or slave when their state entered the Union. It abolished the Missouri Compromise of 1820, which prohibited slavery north and west of 36°30′ latitude. People of all political persuasions throughout the North—Whig, Free Soil, and Democrat—opposed opening the territories to slavery. In early 1854 political leaders across Wisconsin called for meetings to oppose the act. One of these meetings, held at Ripon, Wisconsin, on March 20, 1854, is considered to be a founding meeting of the Republican Party.

On April 25, 1857, *Emigranten* announced, "the newspaper's editorship has as of April 17 been delegated to Mr. C. Fr. Solberg." April 3, 1857, was the last *Emigranten* number dated in Inmansville; the April 20 issue gave Madison, Dane County, Wisconsin, as the place of publication. It was published under the motto "Forward to Truth and Enlightenment" (*Fremad til Sandhed og Oplysning*). The Solberg family moved to America in 1853 when Carl Fredrik Solberg, born in Christiania (Oslo), was twenty years old. He had spent much of his youth in Denmark, where his family lived and his father operated a bakery, and had attended the elite Sorø Academy, where he had studied English. As he himself told it in a 1919 interview, "I thus knew English before coming to America. I had an advantage over many other immigrants."

Carl Fredrik Solberg, owner
and editor of the newspaper
Emigranten. Norwegian-
American Historical
Association

In 1857 as editor and three years later also owner, Solberg strengthened *Emigranten*'s Republican identity. He was clearly the newspaper's most capable editor, and being the proprietor gave him greater
influence. After he purchased the rival Democratic *Nordstjernen* (The
North Star) in October 1859, his was the sole Norwegian-language
newspaper—a sign of the Democratic Party's weakened position
among Norwegian voters in the Northwest. In editorials Solberg depicted Republicans as champions of the distribution of land—of a
homestead act, a popular cause in the West in the 1850s. Solberg
furthermore declared that *Emigranten* wanted to have "no slavery
for either blacks or whites." An increase in subscribers to four thousand in 1860 showed that the Republicans' leading issues and the

question of slavery had the support of Norwegian immigrants. There is much evidence that *Emigranten* participated in and worked for this swing from a Democratic to a Republican direction.[6]

Prospecting for Gold

Hans Christian Heg's talent for politics developed from his teenage years, and he became an active local political worker. He played a role in the religious life of Muskego and the Norwegian American press and influenced and was influenced by both. His father, needless to say, was a central figure. But as Blegen explains, "Politics yielded temporarily . . . to the lure of adventure." On January 24, 1848, James Marshall, as the story goes, uttered the famous words "I have found it." Marshall discovered pieces of gold in the Sacramento Valley by Sutter's sawmill, located at the confluence of the American and Sacramento Rivers. News of the discovery spread quickly and widely. The following year the California gold triggered a massive movement of fortune seekers from the ends of the earth. In the comprehensive book *The Age of Gold*, H. W. Brands affirms that the Gold Rush inspired a new American dream—the "dream of instant wealth, won by audacity and good luck."

On March 26, 1849, *Nordlyset* reported: "Today departed from here (*Idag afreiste herfra*) the brothers Engebret and Halvor Rosvald in the company of Hans Chr. Heg and Magnus Hansen, after their decision to California." Hans Heg, at the age of twenty, and his companions joined the army of forty-niners, the name given prospectors in the California Gold Rush of 1849. The party of four young friends proceeded with their long journey across the continent. Their course and advance west were reported by Heg in letters printed in *Nordlyset*.

Nordlyset described how the four young argonauts started on the overland trek on March 26, well equipped with a solid wagon and two yokes of oxen. The newspaper expressed its confidence that they "should be quite safe on their forthcoming long, inconvenient, and tedious journey," for "as far as human understanding and planning may avail, they have taken every precaution."

Modern-day readers might be incredulous at the thought of cross-country travel with oxen as the propellant. Insight comes from tracing the lengthy and arduous crossing. The party reached Hannibal, Missouri, located along the Mississippi River, on April 6. They thereafter made it across the state to St. Joseph, located on the Missouri River. On April 29, Heg wrote a letter to his brother, Ole, printed in *Nordlyset* on May 17, 1849, in which he complains about the roads and even more about the bridges washed away by ice. Otherwise, he writes, everything went quite well.

The party acquired an additional yoke of oxen and intended soon to buy another. They would thus have four yokes for the long journey westward. They also secured a horse. At St. Joseph they were able to buy at a lower price than in Hannibal—"the reason being," Heg explains, "that there are here quite a few who have become discouraged with the journey and are now selling out at less than half price." It was not an uncommon circumstance.

In a letter to his brother, dated May 2 at Savannah Landings and printed in *Nordlyset* on October 12, Heg relates that they were delayed a few days because of the large crowd of people waiting to cross the Missouri. He assures his brother that their health is good and that they are in fine spirits. And, he writes, the reports from California were exceptionally favorable. They had come to the dividing line between civilization and wilderness. "We are now camped on the banks of the Missouri River," Heg relates, "where on the one side, as far as the eye can penetrate, one sees only the wild Indian land through which our journey goes to California."

After crossing the Missouri, "the little company of gold seekers from Muskego," as Blegen refers to them, made their way to Fort

Laramie, Wyoming, a significant nineteenth-century trading post, and thereafter to Green River, a town named after the river in the south-western part of the state, a distance of four hundred miles.

Heg and party reached South Pass, Wyoming, in the Rocky Mountains, on July 4. They chose the southern route across the Continental Divide. In a letter from Salt Lake City dated July 17, Heg described the South Pass as "the most beautiful road that we ever could wish for."

They arrived at Salt Lake City, Utah, on July 16. There they met Mormon settlers, many of whom had arrived with Brigham Young in 1847. Westward the party followed a route on the north side of Salt Lake. In his letter from Salt Lake City, Heg relates that he had met many Mormons who had been at the gold mines the year before, and "they assured us all that we could find enough gold if we only were able to endure the hard work that is connected with digging and washing out the gold." They reported that ordinarily one is able to make from four hundred to a thousand dollars a week. If accurate, this was comforting news. Such positive information spread widely, and at a time when most people made less than a dollar a day, the California goldfields naturally held great attraction.

After many adventures and hardships, the Wisconsin gold seek-ers arrived safely at their destination, Weaverville, one of three major gold rush towns that formed northern California, on September 14, 1849—174 days, or nearly half a year, after their departure from Mus-kego. In a letter dated October 7, 1849, Hans Christian writes to his brother, Ole, from "my new home" (*mit nye Hjem*) the following: "After a strenuous journey of 174 days from the time we left Muskego, we reached this place, which was the first mine we found—the 14th of September." Writing in Norwegian, Heg describes the process of staking a claim, how to dig for gold, how to pan for gold from a riverbed, adding, "A man can here make 10 to 20 dollars a day"

(*En Mand kan her tjene 10 til 20 Dollars pr. Dag*). He then points to the
high prices on supplies, which reduced the income. All of Heg's letters from California except for one have not been preserved, but they
did appear in the local paper. In one likely written in the spring of
1850, quoted by Knud Langeland in his article "Oberst H. C. Heg"
(Colonel H. C. Heg), Heg gives insight into life in the goldfield. He
and Magnus Hansen had worked together since they arrived in September and had built a log house, ten square feet in size with a good
fireplace. He and Hansen had saved one thousand dollars, besides
expenses, which amounted to about three hundred dollars.

The California Gold Rush attracted hundreds of thousands of ambitious young people from all over the world. Only a few men struck
it rich, however, and many returned home disappointed or settled
and became farmers or found other employment.

In Heg's opinion, "the best part of the gold harvest (*Guldhøsten*)
is now over, and those who come out next year will find themselves
most disappointed." Langeland relates furthermore that after two
years among the gold miners and just beginning to have considerable
success (*gjøre sin Lykke*), Heg received the tragic news from home that
his father, Even Heg, had died on August 17, 1850, after a short illness,
as reported by *Democraten*. His mother, Siri Olsdatter Heg, had died
eight years earlier. Hans Christian Heg's younger siblings—Ole, nine-
teen, Andrea, fifteen, and Sophie, thirteen—needed his care. Heg
consequently returned to Muskego in 1851 to assume charge of the
home farm and be with his brother and two younger sisters.

In the two years Hans Christian Heg spent in California there were
historical transformations on the continent. In 1848 Mexico ceded
California to the United States. The rapid growth in population produced by the Gold Rush made the question of statehood a pressing
matter and dictated that the slavery question would be called there.
Even though California would play a small role in the American

Civil War, a bitter debate occurred between slave-state and free-soil advocates. Heg must have been well aware of the rancor and perhaps even participated in the heated discord. Unfortunately, no record has been preserved. In *Roaring Camp*, Susan Lee Johnson describes white slaveholders bringing enslaved people to the Gold Rush, a disturbing vision, and while defended by slavery proponents this move was attacked by both Northerners and nonslaveholding white Southerners. Abolitionists and antislavery forces were active. On September 9, 1850, California—the thirty-first state—entered the union as a free-labor state.[7]

MARRIAGE AND FAMILY LIFE

Hans Christian Heg inherited the 320-acre farm his father owned by Wind Lake in Racine County. Upon his return he took over and managed the family farm. Farming was his main business, though engaging in politics and war were hardly incidental but strong and enduring commitments, as *The Wisconsin Blue Book* of 1933 states. On December 10, 1851, shortly after his return from the goldfields, Hans Christian Heg, twenty-two, and Gunild Einong, eighteen, were united in marriage. They had likely met in Muskego, where they both grew up.

Four children were born to Hans Christian and Gunild; one daughter, Annetta, died in 1860 at the age of three. Edmund (James E.) Heg was born on September 22, 1852, in Norway, Racine County. The other two children were Hilda Siri Heg Fowler, born on March 2, 1854, also in Norway, Racine County, and Elmer Ellsworth Heg, born on February 22, 1861, in Waupun, Dodge County, Wisconsin.

All three Heg siblings found success in life. James Edmund Heg (generally identified by his middle name) was a newspaperman in Chicago and in Wisconsin. He was a longtime editor of the *Lake Geneva Herald* and served as president of the Wisconsin Press

Hans Christian and Gunild (Einong) Heg. Norwegian-American Historical
Association

Association. He was also for a time a member of the Wisconsin
board of control. James Edmund Heg died on April 6, 1914, at
Waukegan, Illinois. He was buried at Lake Geneva.

Hilda Siri Heg Fowler studied in Germany after earning her degree at Beloit College. She later taught music in a school for girls.
On April 30, 1870, she married Charles N. Fowler, also a graduate of
Beloit College, and later of Yale University. He earned a law degree
in 1878 at the University of Chicago Law School. Fowler was a successful lawyer and a Republican Party politician in New Jersey. Hilda
Fowler died in Orange, New Jersey, on February 20, 1932, and Charles
Fowler the same year on May 27. They were both interred in Fair-
view Cemetery in Westfield, New Jersey.

Elmer Ellsworth Heg was educated at Beloit College and Bellevue
Hospital Medical School of New York. In 1888 he moved to Yakima,
Washington Territory, where he became a prominent physician.
Dr. Heg was appointed Washington territorial doctor by the United

States in 1888, and in 1898–99 he served as brigade surgeon, US Volunteers, in the Spanish-American War. He held senior medical positions in Seattle and the state of Washington, in 1909–11 serving as state health commissioner. After 1909 he was medical director of the Pulmonary Hospital in Seattle. Dr. Heg died September 26, 1922, in Seattle.

In 1859 Heg gave up farming, and he and the family made their home in Waterford in Racine County. In company with two Native Americans, he conducted a mill and general store. Gunild lived with the children in Waterford until she moved to Beloit in Rock County so they could attend Beloit College. Education for the children was the ambition of both Hans Christian and Gunild Heg, and much discussed during his last visit home from the battlefield and in his correspondence.

The year 1859 became a substantial marker in Heg's political career. He had an interest and even some experience in politics before going to California, and it attracted him after his return. His political venture will be more fully dealt with in the following chapter.[8]

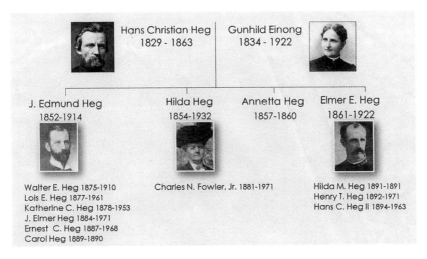

Hans Christian Heg
1829 - 1863

Gunhild Einong
1834 - 1922

J. Edmund Heg
1852-1914

Hilda Heg
1854-1932

Annetta Heg
1857-1860

Elmer E. Heg
1861-1922

Walter E. Heg 1875-1910
Lois E. Heg 1877-1961
Katherine C. Heg 1878-1953
J. Elmer Heg 1884-1971
Ernest C. Heg 1887-1968
Carol Heg 1889-1890

Charles N. Fowler, Jr. 1881-1971

Hilda M. Heg 1891-1891
Henry T. Heg 1892-1971
Hans C. Heg II 1894-1963

Courtesy Lori Coffey

CHAPTER 3

A Venture into Politics

A RISING YOUNG POLITICIAN

In 1851 Hans Christian Heg was twenty-two years old when he returned from the goldfields in California and took over the home farm in Muskego. He already enjoyed the confidence and respect not only of his fellow Norwegian settlers but also of many Native Americans in the vicinity. Heg's taste for politics cannot be said to have totally yielded to "the lure of adventure" to the goldfields, as Theodore C. Blegen claims. The tensions created by the masses of fortune seekers from all parts of the world, and his encounters with both slaveholders and abolitionists and antislavery forces foreshadowed his entry into the political arena upon his return.

Knud Langeland, who knew Hans Heg personally, asserted that Heg's political views were those of the very life of the simple pioneer society of Muskego: "freedom, equality, and the spirit of brotherhood." Slavery was abhorrent to Hans Heg. He naturally became an ardent member of the Free Soil Party, and later of the Republican Party. Blegen agrees: "There can be little doubt that there was a considerable measure of democracy in the pioneer society of Muskego, and it is not difficult to understand why Heg, who seems to have had a sturdy faith in freedom, should have made his political debut as a Free-Soiler."

In 1852 Hans Christian Heg became a Free Soil candidate in Racine
County for a seat in the Wisconsin state assembly; the general election was held on November 2. *Emigranten* for September 12, 1859,
below the heading "Wisconsin Affairs" (*Wisconsin Affærer*), gives a
friendly review of Heg's life and his political engagement. The paper
has little to say about the 1852 election, however, which Heg lost to
the Democratic candidate Thomas West, who was elected by only a
small majority over Heg. Heg's accomplishments in the local political arena receive more attention.[1]

Career in the Town of Norway

The September 12 issue of *Emigranten* actually presents a summary
of Heg's career in local politics. His defeat in state politics led him to
enter into the political and civic work of his own community. "At the
same time," Blegen says, "he won a valuable schooling in practical
politics in those basic units of American government, the township
and the county."

The Town of Norway in Racine County is unique in that it has three
lakes within its boundaries and shares another lake with Muskego.
The large central portion of the town consisted of a great peat marsh,
with Wind Lake on its northwestern edge. As related earlier, it was
only with the Norwegians' arrival in 1839 that farmers began to develop the community. More Norwegians, as well as other Europeans
and some Americans, settled in Norway in the 1840s; by the end of
the decade most of the land had been sold. The Town of Norway was
established on February 11, 1847, by the Territory of Wisconsin—a
year before Wisconsin statehood. In 1850 the town had a population
of 751; 404 of the citizens were of Scandinavian, mostly Norwegian,
birth. By 1860 there were 961 inhabitants, the foreign-born still remaining the majority.

Hans Christian Heg, as commentators frequently state, inherited his father's leadership qualities. In 1852 he was made supervisor in the Town of Norway, and he also became a justice of the peace. No record of Heg's actions as justice of the peace have been located. He functioned as a judicial officer with limited power. Like peace officers in Wisconsin in general, he likely oversaw cases that involved civil controversies, hearing minor criminal complaints and committing offenders. Being an officer of the court would make Heg a noted resident of Racine County.

In 1854 Heg became chairman of the board of supervisors in the Town of Norway, and in 1855 he was reelected to this position. As chairman of the town board Heg was also a member from his district of the Racine County Board, which met at the town of Racine, the county seat. Record books are preserved at the Racine County Courthouse. In these the name of Hans Christian Heg occurs frequently. The minutes of the meetings held during his time show that Heg took an active and intelligent part in the proceedings of the county board. He also served on many important committees.[2]

RACINE COUNTY POOR FARM

The history of the Racine County Poor Farm extends back to 1851, when it was deemed advisable to discontinue the practice of sending the poor, transient, and others in need to the city of Racine to be taken care of. Local governmental units had at this time, by state and territorial statutes, the responsibility for care of their own poor. On September 27 of that year eighty acres of land were deeded by William and Eliza Hunt and subsequently forty more acres were donated by their attorney Ezra Burchard, all to be applied to the same purpose. No action was taken until 1854, however, to support "the medicant and paupers being cared for as of old." In November the board of supervisors decided to erect suitable buildings to accommodate the county poor. The commissioners expedited the construction process, making it possible to open the buildings in January 1855. An asylum building was erected in connection with the poorhouse to handle cases of insanity on the farm.

In 1855 Hans Christian Heg was made one of three commissioners to superintend the Racine County Poor Farm in the western district of the county; John Duffles handled the middle district, and William H. Waterman the eastern. The November 1855 *Journal of Proceedings of the Board of Supervisors* narrates Heg's service on the judiciary committee as poorhouse commissioner, which that year was called to identify the eligible paupers and then report "back to the Board the accounts of the following named persons and recommend their allowances at the following amounts," which are then given. Heg was active in his support of the poor. Becoming commissioner of the Racine County Poor Farm the following year augmented his responsibilities. In 1857 he was reelected as a poorhouse commissioner.

Also in 1857 Hans Heg was occupied with entering state politics and resigned from his post in the Town of Norway. He was greatly satisfied with his brother, Ole Heg, two years his junior, being elected to succeed him. Judging from correspondence between them, the two brothers appear to share political convictions though clearly not the same political drive. Ole Heg learned the printer's trade growing up in Muskego, with the publication of *Nordlyset*, and later settled down in the printing business.

The proceedings of the Racine County Board make clear that the supervisors were concerned that too much money was spent on poor relief and tried to cut expenditures. The drive for economy was perhaps legitimate, considering the high proportion of the county's budget consumed in support of the poor, even though cutting expenses negatively affected individual paupers' needs. Hans Heg was likely familiar with the poor relief system in Norway from childhood memories and even more from reflecting on the compassion his father Even Heg had shown for "the burdensome poor," and the high poor relief tax he had paid. These recollections likely affected Hans Christian Heg's own mission as poor farm commissioner.

The published annual proceedings of the board of supervisors clearly reveal Hans Heg as a most active member. There is also much evidence of his empathy and concern for Racine County's indigent citizens in the motions he offers and in his voting record. Commenting on his early career as officeholder in Racine County, Blegen concludes: "With the faithful and successful execution of the duties of the various local offices that he held he gained the confidence of increasing numbers of citizens." Heg's biographer agrees.[3]

WISCONSIN STATE POLITICS

In 1859 Hans Christian Heg again entered state politics, and this time with great success. As Knud Langeland boastfully writes: "Mr. Heg became the first Norwegian in America who occupied (*beklædte*) a state office, and it was first then that his name became well known to the people in the state." He was elected on the Republican ticket, and his political campaign and election will be considered later in this chapter. A brief survey of Wisconsin state politics and the Republican Party of Wisconsin will help clarify social and political circumstances that impacted the outcome.

The Republican Party of Wisconsin was founded at a mass state convention in Madison on July 13, 1854, shortly after the genesis of the national Republican Party at Ripon, Wisconsin, on March 20. The state party was symbolically founded on the anniversary of the Northwest Ordinance of 1787 banning slavery in the Northwest Territory. In an 1859 campaign address Heg reminisced about the beautiful land Norwegians were leaving to come to America because it was a free country "whose principles struck a responsive chord in their hearts." Heg then declared: "I was aboard the Republican ship when she was launched . . . [and] so long as she sails under true Republican colors, you can rely upon finding me among the working members of the crew."

By 1859 Norwegians as well as many Germans would agree with Heg, but that was clearly not the case at the time the Republican Party emerged. There then existed among many Germans and Scandinavians a belief that the Republican Party was marred by the Know-Nothing element in Wisconsin. The Norwegian newspaper *Den norske Amerikaner* (The Norwegian American), founded as a fiercely Democratic organ by Elias Stangeland in Madison on January 1, 1855, supported this damaging image. In 1856, by this time edited by Charles M. Reese, the paper attacked *Emigranten*—which in 1854 had moved from the Democratic to the Republican Party—and the Wisconsin Republican Party. The Republican Party was, in *Den norske Amerikaner*'s strong opinion, infested with Whigs, abolitionists, disgruntled Democrats, and Know-Nothings. The newspaper even combined the names as the Republican Know-Nothing Party, even though there was no evidence of an understanding between the Republican and Know-Nothing organizations. In 1855 the Know-Nothing Party chose to support the Republican nominees rather than offer an independent ticket. Shortly before the election the *Milwaukee American* (a Know-Nothing organ) announced that the "Americans" would vote the Republican ticket, because it found the Democratic ticket unworthy of support, while they in general were satisfied with the Republican candidates. This move convinced the public, and especially the foreign-born, that the Republican Party was deeply tainted with a political philosophy they both feared and hated. This feeling declined after 1855, but it was slow to disappear. At state conventions in 1855, both the Democrats and the Republicans passed resolutions denouncing Know-Nothingism. "During [only] a single political canvass," writes Joseph Schafer, "that of 1855, did the Know-Nothing organization figure prominently and in a manner to render its influence calculable." In 1856 the Know-Nothing Party fell apart. *Emigranten*, the most influential of the Republican Norwegian newspapers, defended the Republican Party from attacks such as the one made by *Den norske Amerikaner*. In its January 8, 1857, number *Emigranten* stated editorially: "Our opponents have used as criticism against us that we in 1854 left the 'democratic' party and later have worked in union with the Republicans."

The Know-Nothing Party, byname of the American Party, a nativistic political organization that flourished in the 1850s, was an outgrowth of the strong anti-immigrant and even more anti–Roman Catholic sentiment that began to manifest in the 1840s. A rising tide of immigrants in the 1850s seemed to pose a threat to the economic and political security of native-born Protestant Americans. At its national convention as early as 1845 the Know-Nothing Party had complained about the advance of the ratio of foreign-born to American-born in the country. If the advance continued at the same pace, the fear was that in fifteen years it "will leave the natives of the soil in a minority in their own land." In 1860, when Wisconsin celebrated its twelfth year of statehood, the population had climbed to 775,881, a major gain from 1850, when state residents numbered 470,490. More than a third of the state's population in 1860 was of foreign birth. Germans were the largest group to settle in Wisconsin in the nineteenth century, according to the 1870 census, by then numbering more than 160,000, and indeed were the largest group of European immigrants in the United States. The Irish constituted another major group. *The Wisconsin Blue Book*, 1962, has for 1860 twenty thousand Norwegians, considered a substantial immigrant population.

In the mid-1850s the Norwegian element in Wisconsin was flock-
ing to support the Republican Party. "The great majority of the
Germans," attorney and historian Ernest Bruncken explains, "notwithstanding their entire lack of sympathy with the slave-holders,
remained Democratic until the outbreak of the War of Secession and
even longer." The Republican Party appeared to many Germans to be
hostile to foreign-born citizens, while the Democrats accepted their
customs and were willing to allow them to take part in all the political rights and privileges of the native-born. As the slavery system
assumed greater public attention, more and more Germans became
disappointed with how the Democratic Party treated that issue, and
Republicanism steadily gained ground among the Germans. In their
platforms of 1857 both political parties declared against nativism
with great emphasis.

Both political parties sought the vote of the foreign-born. According to the Wisconsin state constitution of 1848, white men of foreign
birth twenty-one years or older were eligible to vote by declaring
their intention to become citizens of the United States. The foreign
voters held the balance of power in Wisconsin. Blegen notes that
"political recognition of racial groups was forwarded by the desire of
politicians to erect buffers against charges of nativism." Hans Christian Heg's winning candidacy on the Republican ticket in 1859 may
at least in part be understood in this context. His nomination would
appeal to the Scandinavian voters. And he was by then recognized
for his leadership and responsibility. In the autumn of 1857 Heg had
been a delegate from Racine County to the Republican state convention in Madison. *Emigranten*, dated September 16, 1857, editorially rating the 1857 state convention, highlights how the newspaper
had encouraged Norwegians to "get one of ours on the state ticket."
It was regretful, *Emigranten* concluded, that no Scandinavian showed
any interest for politics, "as the only delegate at the convention the

Scandinavians had sent there was our countryman Mr. Hans C. Heg, who represented the Norwegian voters in Racine County." Though unprepared, as *Emigranten* states, Heg after strong encouragement from a group of Norwegians in Madison consented (*samtykkede*) to become a candidate for state office. His nomination would recognize the Norwegian element in Wisconsin. At this juncture, in competition with other candidates, Heg secured only a few votes, and thus did not earn the nomination.

Two years later Hans Heg again entered state politics. The Republican state convention met in Madison at the turn of the months August–September 1859. His nomination for prison commissioner (*Statsfængselsinspektør*), made by the delegate from Dane County, was recounted in *Emigranten*, September 5, 1859. There was evidently much enthusiasm, as the paper reported: "A multitude of delegates shouted Hans Heg! Heg! Heg! Is the man." He got a substantial majority of the votes. A committee was appointed to inform Heg about the nomination, but he was not in town and only learned of it later.

Heg accepted the nomination and entered a successful campaign, during which he traveled about in the state; he made political addresses emphasizing the slavery issue, speaking Norwegian to Norwegian settlements and English elsewhere. Heg considered his nomination a compliment to the Norwegians, and he convincingly maintained—as described in *Emigranten,* October 10, 1859—in his campaign speeches that the Republicans were not nativistic. In a strong endorsement of Heg, *Emigranten,* September 12, gives a detailed account of Heg's life experience, even including his gold prospecting as evidence of a high degree of courage, strong determination, and a powerful and robust body (*kraftigt og haardført Legeme*). The editorial stresses his antislavery conviction as the main feature (*Hovedtrækk*) of his policy. *Emigranten* concluded its endorsement by assuring its readers that when elected, Heg would administer his position in an honorable manner, lending Norwegians pride in having a countryman as a member of the state government. *Emigranten* for September 26 cites the *Racine Journal*'s endorsement of September 14 and the journal's claim that there are only a few Norwegians who will have anything to do with the Democratic Party. Norwegians in Heg's own community thus had great confidence in him as a Republican candidate and, according to *Emigranten*, all American Republican newspapers in the state offered a favorable and honorable mention of Heg—something, the paper contends, the state's Norwegian Democratic organs did not like very much.

The campaign made Heg well known throughout the state of Wisconsin—a significant achievement as he considered his political career. In the election on November 8, he received a majority of 2,673 votes over his Democratic opponent, Henry C. Fleck, who, like Heg, was Norwegian, presumably nominated to appeal to Norwegian voters. Heg thus attained the office of state prison commissioner. In addition, Heg evidently earned the distinction of being the first Norwegian immigrant elected to a state office in the United States.

In a lettter written in Norwegian and published in *Stavanger Amtstidende* on July 18, 1861, Hans Christian Heg reviews his entry into state politics and election as prison commissioner:

> At a convention the fall of 1857, I was called by the Norwegians to be a candidate for the post of inspector of the state prison; but that time I did not get the nomination. At the Republican state convention the fall of 1859 I was nominated for the previously reported post without I myself knowing anything about it, and nor did I wish such an appointment, as I then was occupied with several important businesses of my own; nevertheless I accepted the nomination and was elected by a majority close to 3,000 votes more than my [Democratic]

opponent, Mr. Henry Fleck, also a Norwegian, I took possession of the position for two years on January 1, 1860.[4]

STATE PRISON COMMISSIONER

Shortly after statehood, Wisconsin authorized a state prison to be built at Waupun, chosen because of the abundance of limestone for construction. Waupun, founded in 1839, is located in Dodge and Fond du Lac Counties. The state prison opened in July 1851 and housed both adult men and adult women. The main building was erected in 1854.

Heg's description of the state prison he had been elected to supervise provides a better understanding of the personal challenges and responsibilities he encountered:

> I must now give you a brief insight into what I am in charge of. The prison is located in the city of Waupun, about 65 English miles northwest of Milwaukee. We have at present 156 prisoners, of whom 27 are lifetime prisoners. This is a smaller number [prisoners] than usual, which from time to time has been 200. I have full management of the prison and about 20 men as guards and so on. The prisoners are for the most part occupied with work on the buildings, the brick walls, and partly factory work. My salary is about 1,500 dollars annually.

Emigranten showed a constant interest in Hans Heg and his administration of the prison. In two issues the newspaper carried accounts titled "A Visit to Wisconsin's State Prison" (*En Tur til Wisconsins Statsfængsel*) by Carl Fredrik Solberg, *Emigranten*'s publisher and editor. The first installment presents a detailed description of buildings and prison inventory, including a church served by a Methodist pastor. The concluding paragraph relates how the cells were furnished, Heg giving permission to have the prisoner's pictures and paintings on the walls. Heg is praised for dealing with the prisoners with the greatest kindness and humanity, which, as Heg saw it, was best both for the state and for the prisoners. As a contrasting example, a former commissioner who retired in 1858 ruled with an iron hand, putting a large number of prisoners in chains, something that was rare during Heg's administration.

In the second installment in *Emigranten*, Solberg gives a detailed account of daily life in the prison. It is characterized by military precision. The inmates are awakened by a large clock at five, given breakfast in their cells at six; at seven all the cell doors open simultaenously and the inmates step out. They line up in front of the main building and in groups follow their keepers to their work. A number of the keepers, Solberg notes, are Norwegian. The guards shout instructions. There are shoemaker and tailor shops, inmates making furniture, others working outside on building a sewer, or employed on the prison farm. The few women inmates, housed separately from the male inmates, are occupied sewing, even making hats for the men.

The prisoners conduct their work in silence and do not dare speak to each other or move from their place without the keeper's order or permission. At twelve they return to their cells for dinner (*Middag*), served on tin plates. They pass an hour in their cells before returning to work. The evening clock rings at six, and their day's work is over. In the same way as for other meals, they receive their evening meal (*Aftensmad*) and are locked into their cells for the night.

On Sunday the inmates receive clean underwear, a towel, and a sheet from the cell servants. At ten the church clock rings and the prisoners are ward by ward taken in military order by their keepers to the church, where they are seated according to ward. The women are then guided in by a matron. After being joined by quite a number of city people who attend the service, the doors are closed. Solberg makes a point of the pastor being a Methodist, and thus offering special and unfamiliar teachings that he thought suitable for the listeners.

After the church service, the prisoners are given their dinner to take with them to their cells. Then the cell servants pay a visit with a catalog of library holdings. Each inmate can choose a book and have it until the following Sunday. Every fourth Sunday the inmates can write letters. These are delivered to the commissioner, who will mail them depending on acceptable content. Letters and other matters relating to the prisoners were in the same way in the commissioner's hands.

Hans Heg clearly had administrative ability and a deep interest in the perplexity of human conduct and behavior. Heg made many important reforms and improvements, as Langeland relates in *Det Skandinaviske Regiments Historie*, including upgrading the system of prison labor through a workshop for the inmates, with machineries and other appropriate appliances. Langeland considered the workshop the most important reform. Heg in addition had a large drain built from the prison farm, which provided cleaner water and overall greater cleanliness, thus improving the state of health there.

Heg's first report to Governor Alexander W. Randall as state prison commissioner is dated October 1, 1860. Covering the period from January 2, it is to a high degree a financial account of the prison's earnings and expenses. Heg's report supports Langeland's praise of the workshop: in 1860 Heg established on "a firm basis the boot and shoe and cabinet shops, and also opened a cooper shop, and a shop for manufacturing brooms." The work in these shops provided revenue toward supporting the prison, but Heg also viewed it as a means of educating life members and inmates under long sentences in trades of value to the state. Heg maintained that the work of many of the confined convicts would compare favorably with articles manufactured elsewhere, and he urged state institutions to let the state prison provide boots and shoes, clothing, furniture, and other items. Heg lists as potential recipients the reform school and asylum, both already having patronized the prison liberally, and adds to these the "Blind, and Deaf and Dumb Asylums." The ability to make marketable products is explained in Heg's letter to W. H. Watson dated May 7, 1861, in which he offered the convict labor at Waupun to make uniforms. "I have three good cutters in the institution (convicts)," Heg reassured Watson, and he could get assistance as needed from tailors in town. "If you will send me the cloth, measures and necessary instruction, I think we can get up as good uniforms as anybody," and "We are ready to take hold at any time."

The annual report for 1861, dated September 30, covers the period from October 1, 1860. Heg introduced the report by claiming: "The year now closing has been strongly characterized on the part of the convicts, by quiet industry and cheerful obedience." The report reveals Heg's positive and humanistic regard for convicted felons and how society should consider their criminal behavior. Heg maintained that experience had confirmed his certainty "that a mild and merciful application of the rules of discipline is sufficient in all cases to reduce the most hardened offender to obedience—that however deeply steeped in iniquity and hardened in sin, there is still a tender point in the human heart which can be reached by proper management, and the Christian principles of kindness." He furthermore claimed that the civilized world has acknowledged that prisons were not established simply for punishment of offenders but as far as possible "they should be made to reclaim the wandering and save the lost."

Two more statements by Heg indicate his faith in humanity and the purpose of imprisonment. "The penalty of the law," he maintained, "is justly due to its transgressor, but in the midst of deserved wrath, it is God-like to be merciful." He also believed "that cruel infliction . . . in all cases they tend to make a good man bad, and a bad man worse—while nothing will arouse the virtuous aspirations of a fallen man so powerfully as the conviction that it still lies in his power to regain the rights he has forfeited, and that he yet can be respected as a fellow man."

Heg's administration of the state prison was rated high in respect to honesty, efficiency, and economy. His renomination was clearly secured. However, the year 1861 marked the conclusion of Heg's services as prison commissioner. His name was presented for renomination in the state Republican convention, but other duties awaited Heg, and he engaged in the recruiting of Scandinavians for service in the Civil War.[5]

THE BOOTH CASE

The Booth case, as it became known, is Wisconsin's most famous instance of breaking the Fugitive Slave Act. It also gave evidence of Heg's strong abolitionist convictions. Sherman Miller Booth, a temperance lecturer, abolitionist, political campaigner, and editor, was born in Davenport, New York, in 1812. His experience and schooling before moving to Wisconsin prepared him well for his antislavery and abolitionist calling in the state. Among his many achievements was his role in organizing the Liberty Party in New Haven, Connecticut, an abolitionist party born from the evangelical American and Foreign Anti-Slavery Society. Booth graduated from Yale University in 1841, and the following year he became the party's agent in Connecticut, where he worked with Ichabod Codding editing the *Christian Freeman*.

In May 1848, just before Wisconsin became a state, Booth accompanied Codding to the territory. There he took charge of the abolitionist paper the *American Freeman*, moving it from Waukesha, the county seat of Waukesha County, to Milwaukee. He soon became

Sherman Miller Booth, influential antislavery activist and abolitionist.
Wisconsin Historical Society

the publisher, changing the name to the *Wisconsin Freeman* and, later, to the *Daily Free Democrat*. He published the periodical until 1859.

The Fugitive Slave Act became the most hated and openly violated federal legislation in the nation's history. Booth and Heg became major actors in resisting and violating the law. Passed by the US Congress and then signed into law by President Millard Fillmore on September 18, 1850, it was part of the Compromise of 1850 between Southern interests in slavery and Northern Free Soilers. The new law was not accepted as a compromise, but fueled the flames of antislavery sentiment. Federal officers were responsible for capturing runaways, and the law penalized officials who did not arrest someone allegedly escaping from slavery. The law required that, upon capture, all escaped enslaved people be returned to the slave owner. Southern slave catchers used dogs to track down fugitives from slavery. Any person aiding a fugitive by providing food or shelter was subject to six months imprisonment and a fine of $1,000. Officers who captured a fugitive from slavery, on the other hand, were entitled to a bonus.

In the spring of 1852, an enslaved man named Joshua Glover from St. Louis escaped from a Missouri plantation and made his way to Racine, where he found work in a sawmill. Missourian slave hunters arrived in the state. Two years later, on the night of March 10, 1854, Glover was seized in his shack by five men headed by his former master, Bennami Garland, and a federal marshal. Glover was forced into the back of a wagon and taken to jail in Milwaukee, where he was held pending a hearing.

The next morning, as word of the capture quickly spread, Booth was informed by telegram. He was soon to make Glover's arrest Wisconsin's news of the decade. The writ of habeas corpus issued by a justice of the court to seize Glover would not stand. Booth is said to have mounted his horse and galloped through the streets of

Poster offering $600 for the return of three runaway slaves in Calvert County, Maryland, dated April 19, 1849. Wisconsin Historical Society

Milwaukee shouting: "Freemen! To the rescue! Slave catchers are in our midst! Be at the courthouse at 2 p.m. in protest!" A crowd of nearly five thousand gathered, about one hundred of them arriving by boat from Racine. Booth encouraged them to show their outrage. After Booth made a fiery speech, the restless mob, led by one of the other committeemen, Johan Ryecraft, battered down the jail door and freed Glover. He spent many nights in fear that he would be captured again. Many men and women risked everything they had to defy the Fugitive Slave Act and keep Joshua Glover safe. After nearly forty days on the run, he was put aboard a steamer in Racine headed to Canada. Glover spent the rest of his life in Canada as a free man and lived the life he chose for himself. Three days after freeing Glover from jail, Booth declared in the *Daily Free Democrat* that the Fugitive Slave Act had been effectively repealed in Wisconsin.

Booth was arrested and charged by federal authorities with assisting Glover's escape, and thus violating the Fugitive Slave Act. The impasse placed Booth in the center of a six-year controversy between state and federal authorities that eventually reached the US Supreme Court. The law brought the issue home to antislavery citizens in the North, as it made them and their institutions responsible for enforcing slavery. Researcher Kevin Dier-Zimmel reports that federal marshal Stephen Ableman started a long period of litigations against Booth, beginning with the 1854 rescue of Glover. Booth withstood "19 trials running 13 years, was fined twice, imprisoned three times and spent $35,000 for his defense"—all linked to dramatic state and federal conflicts and incidents.

Regardless of legal obstacles, Booth endured. He continued his battle against the slave law. From prison Booth appealed again and again to the Wisconsin Supreme Court. On February 3, 1855, in a decision unique to Wisconsin, the court declared the Fugitive Slave Act unconstitutional, resulting in Booth's release. The US Supreme

The Joshua Glover Commemorative Marker was designated in Racine, Wisconsin, on June 7, 2001, by the National Park Service and is part of the Racine Underground Railroad Freedom Heritage Trail. A board alongside the marker notes that it "commemorates Glover and the citizens of Racine who, at their peril, aided one of their own out of the bondage of slavery." Photo by Christopher Paulson, executive director, Racine Heritage Museum

Court agreed to hear the case, but the state court's refusal to trans-
mit its decision to Washington delayed it for four years. On March 7,
1859, Chief Justice Roger Taney, speaking for a unanimous US
Supreme Court, rejected the position of the state rights' advocates,
reversed the Wisconsin Supreme Court, and declared the Fugitive
Slave Act constitutional. The end of the slave law occurred in August
1861, when the US Congress enacted the Confiscation Act, which
barred enslavers from re-enslaving captured fugitives; the Fugitive
Slave Act was formally repealed in June 1864.

Booth continued to suffer legal controversies. On March 1, 1860,
the US attorney in Milwaukee, D. A. J. Upham, had Booth rearrested
and placed in federal custody in Milwaukee for not having paid his
fine nor served the jail time imposed following his conviction in
federal court after his rescue of Glover. Booth's short term in prison
expired, but he remained confined in the federal customhouse in
Milwaukee because he refused to pay his fines.

On August 1, 1860, a group of armed men forcibly rescued Booth
from the federal customhouse in Milwaukee and took him to Waupun, where prison commissioner Hans C. Heg gave him protection.
In several issues of *Waupun Prison City Newspaper* and *Waupun Times*,
Heg reports on Booth's presence. On August 10, 1860, the prison
newspaper has the following account: "It is true, that on Booth's
arrival in Waupun he called at the office of the Commissioner, and
was politely received, and in a friendly manner invited to the hos-
pitalities of the Commissioner, and accordingly became the guest of
Major Heg." *Waupun Times*, August 5, 1860, printed Heg's response
to the US marshal's warrant of arrest of Booth and request to surrender him to the marshal's custody. Heg rejected the request by
assuring the marshal that Booth was not secreted but simply visiting
him and at liberty to go wherever he pleased. "As to rendering you
assistance to aid you in his arrest," Heg concluded, "allow me politely

to say that force is at present employed in a more profitable and honorable way."

Booth continued to speak at numerous political meetings in the area. Finally, on October 8, 1860, Booth was recaptured by federal marshals at a meeting in Berlin, Wisconsin, and taken back to the customhouse in Milwaukee. After Abraham Lincoln's election but before the inauguration, Booth applied to President James Buchanan for a pardon. On the day before Lincoln's inauguration on March 4, 1861, Buchanan pardoned Booth.[6]

THE UNDERGROUND RAILROAD

Joshua Glover, Wisconsin's best-known fugitive, was hardly alone in being transported and saved through the Underground Railroad. In analyzing the Fugitive Slave Act, Arlow W. Andersen makes the point that it "was all but nullified in effect by the enactment of personal liberty laws in Northern states, by moral resentment on the part of many who were not out-and-out abolitionists, and by active countermeasures well exemplified in the mysterious workings of the Underground Railroad"—a system of homes abolitionists used to help freedom seekers make their way to safety.

A historical essay titled "The Underground Railroad in Wisconsin" states that between 1842 and 1861 Wisconsin residents helped more than one hundred runaway enslaved people escape to freedom in Canada. The details of how fugitives passed through Wisconsin are scarce, however, because both the enslaved and their helpers had to conceal their work. Anyone who helped enslaved fugitives escape was subject to heavy penalties.

Racine County's involvement in the Underground Railroad is documented from 1842. The earliest recorded escape is that of sixteen-year-old Caroline Quarles (Quarlls), who ran away from her enslaver in St. Louis, Missouri, on July 4, 1842, after being beaten. She came up the Mississippi River by steamboat to Alton, Illinois, and crossed by stage to Milwaukee, where she arrived in early August, secretly helped by Wisconsin abolitionists. Her experience reveals the real threat of being caught and prosecuted, the long ordeal, and the many obstacles faced by fleeing enslaved people, as well as the essential aid given by those opposed to slavery.

In August 1842 the Samuel Brown farm in Milwaukee served as a stop on the Underground Railroad during Caroline Quarles's escape. Brown thought it imperative that a young freedom seeker be conveyed to railroads. She was hidden by sympathetic allies in Milwaukee until authorities tracked her down; then she was spirited away to Pewaukee, where she hid for two weeks, and to Waukesha, a town known for its antislavery radicals. In late summer she moved at night from farm to farm through Walworth and Racine Counties. Lyman Goodnow from Waukesha ultimately drove the wagon that took her by night on an extended and arduous excursion around Chicago, through Indiana, and across Michigan, where she escaped from Detroit into Canada. Goodnow wrote a long and detailed memoir about the episode.

Achas P. Dutton, a resident of Racine, was a major Underground Railroad conductor and had a role in the escape of Joshua Glover and about one hundred others. His warehouses along the south bank of the Root River in Racine were concealment and embarkation sites. Dutton provided a link to the Great Lakes portion of the Underground Railroad. He transferred freedom seekers to the vessels of abolition-friendly lake captains, who transported them to Canadian ports and freedom. In Racine escapees could embark safely on steamers for Canada. Dutton estimated that more than a hundred went by boat from Racine alone in the years before the Civil War. A monument on the south side of the Root River in Racine commemorates Dutton's role in the maritime connection of the Underground Railroad.

Achas P. Dutton was a major Underground Railroad conductor in Racine. Racine Heritage Museum

The site has official designation as part of the National Underground Railroad Network to Freedom.

Following the Civil War, in spite of the racism that permeated American society and made many fearful of speaking about their role as slave liberators before the war, Dutton and Maximillian Heck, both of Racine, admitted that between 1854 and 1861 a number of the city's residents conspired to help fugitive enslaved people board steamers bound for Ontario. They frequently took up collections to cover their expenses. Most of those transported had come up the Illinois River to Chicago and then overland to Kenosha, Racine, or Milwaukee. Others came up the Rock River to Beloit, and then to Milton, where the Milton House provided another safe location. They likely then were transported across the prairie to find voyage to Canada from Racine or another lake port.

Several locations in southern Wisconsin served as stops on the Underground Railroad. Milton House—a certified designated state historic site—once a stagecoach station and inn, was a popular stop for travelers because of its location near prominent roadways and its proximity to the Rock River, which, as indicated above, played an important part in the route to freedom for fleeing enslaved people.

Joseph Goodrich, founder of the village of Milton in 1839 and proprietor of the Milton House, was a Seventh Day Baptist from western New York. Milton House was opened in 1845; as many as twenty to thirty coaches per day were stopping at the Milton House in the early years, prompting an expansion. Goodrich and his family were conductors on the Underground Railroad and used their property to hide fugitives. Goodrich, through political alliances and personal lobbying, brought the Milwaukee and Mississippi Railroad through Milton. Railroads facilitated the passage of fugitives; some railroad companies led by antislavery men did so as a matter of policy. Wisconsin was the leading state in the west of the antislavery movement from 1840 until the Civil War. Goodrich and the Milton House represent an important regional expression of the national abolition movement.

As the destination for freedom-seeking enslaved people, Canada may be considered the Promised Land. In *Bound for Canaan*, the epic story of the Underground Railroad, Fergus Bordewich places the history of what he describes as "America's First Civil Rights Movement" in a broad national context. "The equality of all souls before God" was stressed from the late 1600s by evangelical Methodists and Baptists. But it was the Quakers who dominated in the early phase of the antislavery movement well into the nineteenth century. The Quaker-led Pennsylvania Abolition Society was uncompromising in its opposition to slavery, morally committed to emancipation, and pragmatic in its determination to put fugitives beyond the reach of their former masters.

The National Underground Railroad Network to Freedom designated "Racine's Underground Railroad Maritime Link" on June 10, 2005. Photo by Christopher Paulson, executive director, Racine Heritage Museum

In considering the history of slavery in the United States, the early opposition to it and efforts to free fellow enslaved humans give a more nuanced impression of the institution. The bloody uprising in Virginia on August 13, 1831, led by the enslaved Nat Turner, is described as a seismic shift. Turner was executed, as were up to two hundred African Americans in retribution, most of them guilty of no wrongdoing. Turner's insurrection effectively put an end to any support for emancipation in the South. It led directly to ever worse restrictions on Blacks and also on whites who publicly challenged the institution of slavery.

Through the 1820s only in southeastern Pennsylvania was there anything resembling the Underground Railroad. In 1825 Philadelphians were shocked to learn that a kidnapping ring had operated in the city for years, luring young Black children onto sloops moored in the Delaware River and shipping them into the Deep South, where they were sold. It was a repugnant trade affecting Northern states. The kidnapping of free Blacks prompted the passage of new laws in the 1820s that gradually made it easier for abolitionists to aid fugitives with less risk to themselves. This legal umbrella sheltered the early phases of underground activity.

In December 1833, delegates arrived in Philadelphia for the first national conference of abolitionists in the country's history. The conference was the idea of William Lloyd Garrison, who the previous year had founded the Boston-based New England Anti-Slavery Society. The delegates were mostly young and mainly from New York, New England, and Pennsylvania. They issued a declaration stating that freedom must be unconditional and that all persons of color ought to be immediately granted the same privileges as other Americans.

The American Anti-Slavery Society, built on Garrison's model, founded in 1833, undertook massive national effort to carry out what a later generation would term "consciousness raising" to convert white

Americans to immediate emancipation, according to Bordewich. It never advocated breaking the law, although it refused to censure any of its members who assisted enslaved people in their escapes. And, Bordewich maintains, there were countless abolitionists who refused to break federal law.

The Underground Railroad and the abolitionist movement as a whole were never completely congruent. There were active members of the underground, including at least some Democrats, who never joined any formal organization. A widespread disillusion with national parties fostered the Underground Railroad's growth as more and more Americans became willing to break laws they believed to be sinful but impossible to change by political means. The underground expanded rapidly, and nowhere more so than in the Ohio River valley. Once across the river and having made contact with the underground, fugitives were regularly passed to safety from town to town and from farm to farm all the way to the Great Lakes. In many of the river communities underground work was carried out almost entirely by African Americans.

The Underground Railroad was not, as often visualized, a fixed system that once established was rarely altered. In reality, routes were always in flux. Even as new routes were opened, old ones became too dangerous or were no longer practical and were abandoned. Bordewich makes the point that the growth of the underground network occurred almost precisely at the same time as the expansion of iron railroads, "which were," he concludes, "transforming the physical and psychological landscape of America as dramatically as the abolitionist movement was changing the country's moral landscape."[7]

THE WIDE AWAKES AND THE ELECTION OF 1860

When Hans Christian Heg, as reported in *Waupun Times* on August 5, 1860, spoke of his "force," he was not simply speaking of those under his command as prison commissioner. Heg also had a second command as first captain of the Waupun company of the "Wide Awakes," a recently formed abolitionist club organized in every state of the North to defend against trespass by Southern slave hunters. The Wide Awakes were a youth organization and later a paramilitary organization cultivated by the Republican Party during the 1860 presidential election. During the four-way race for president, the six-year-old Republican Party found support from a new generation of voters who helped push Abraham Lincoln to victory.

They were known as the Wide Awakes because of their youth, enthusiasm, and torchlit nighttime marches. While campaigning for Lincoln, William H. Seward, soon to become secretary of state, claimed, "Now the old men are folding their arms and going to sleep and the young men are Wide Awake." The historical record shows that the Wide Awakes began to assemble in Hartford, Connecticut, on the night of February 25, 1860. Cassius Clay, an antislavery politician from Kentucky, spoke. A group of young men forming a parade by torchlight escorted him. In March of that year Abraham Lincoln also spoke in Hartford; he proclaimed against the spread of slavery and advocated for the right of workers to strike. After the speech, Wide Awakes, like earlier with Clay, gave Lincoln a torchlight escort back to the hotel. During the following weeks, the Lincoln campaign made plans to develop Wide Awakes throughout the country to spearhead voter registration.

The movement grew quickly in the spring and summer, with clubs forming across the North and Midwest. Chicago had forty-eight clubs alone. By the middle of the 1860s campaign, Republicans bragged that they had Wide Awake chapters in every county of every Northern free state. On the day of Lincoln's election as president, the Wide Awakes had grown to 500,000 members. In Chicago on October 3, 1860, ten thousand Wide Awakes marched in a three-mile procession. The story of the rally occupied eight columns of the *Chicago Tribune*. In Boston, Lincoln's running mate, Hannibal Hamlin, marched through the streets with the young Wide Awakes. On the same date as the procession in Chicago, a huge torchlit procession and pyrotechnic displays dazzled New York City. Tens of thousands came out.

The national organization of the Wide Awakes is not well known, and perhaps a formal governing body did not exist at all. Apparently, the clubs were organized by a city into local chapters. There are surviving minutes of the Waupun chapter under Heg's command. These show that membership was restricted to males eighteen and older. The member had to acquire the style of uniform the club adopted. The Waupun chapter had a military-style officer system consisting of a captain and first to fourth lieutenants.

In an article in the *Journal of American History* published in 2009 at the bicentennial of Abraham Lincoln's birth, historian Jon Grinspan explores the influence of the Wide Awakes' campaign. He does not think Wide Awakes themselves made much difference in the election. Even though their actions drew thousands of voters to the polls, Grinspan is of the opinion that Lincoln would have won without the movement. He argues instead that they helped create focus in the muddled political times and stirred up the enthusiasm of other voters. Grinspan concludes: "By the end of 1860, the nation was wide awake."[8]

CHAPTER 4

⸙

The Fifteenth
Wisconsin Regiment

INTRODUCTION

The years leading up to hostilities between the North and the South engendered social, political, and moral discord nationwide in regard to slavery, state rights versus federal authority, and secession from the Union. It was also a period of extraordinary increases in immigration. The rise of mass immigration occurred in the years between 1815 and 1860, steadily gathering momentum during the 1830s and 1840s and reaching its crest in 1854. Five million immigrants arrived in the period 1815–60, three million arriving in the single decade 1845–54. There was no precedent for a movement of this magnitude. In this pre–Civil War population shift, while all of Europe was represented, the vast majority of the immigrants came from regions north of the Alps and west of the River Elbe. They settled primarily in the Northern free states, building large rural settlements and urban colonies of European immigrants throughout the region.

Naturally, these new immigrants had an impact on American society and culture. Their engagement in the Civil War represents a major theme of the current chapter. The foreign-born enlisted in the war in great numbers: roughly a quarter to a third of the Union Army consisted of foreign-born men. They for the most part enlisted in regular Union military units, some of which were ethnic regiments. The Fifteenth Wisconsin Regiment, led by Colonel Hans Christian Heg, was hailed as the Norwegian Regiment and can be taken as a representative of ethnic military organizations.

Historian William Burton includes the Fifteenth Wisconsin Regiment in his study *Melting Pot Soldiers*; he covers a number of other ethnicities as well as multiethnic units and has separate chapters on German and Irish regiments. Though a fine study, the use of the metaphor "melting pot" is unfortunate. Burton makes clear in the foreword that he is not adopting the implications of seeing America as a melting pot. The term "melting pot" came into general usage with the publication in 1908 of Israel Zangwill's play *The Melting Pot*, which perpetuated the American ideal of a homogeneous society of many cultures. America is seen as a "crucible" or "melting pot" where immigrant cultures and identities are melted together like metals at great heat to produce a new and common American cultural compound.

A broader discussion of differing views and interpretations of the metaphor is not required in order to focus on a specific thesis. The loss of ethnic identity and culture the "melting pot" concept implies—that is, "Americanization"—dominated American scholarship until the 1960s, when the new social history became the standard. There is no doubt that immigrants responded to the call of patriotism and demand for manpower during the Civil War, and adjusted to life in America and showed loyalty to their adopted homeland. The immigrants and their descendants engaged in dynamic social interaction with dominant American social groups and a multitude of ethnic cultures and nationalities. And yet, Norwegian Americans, for example, did not easily lose their cultural identity through assimilation. The mustering of a Norwegian regiment, the Fifteenth Wisconsin, and the persistent commemorations of the regiment and of Colonel Hans Christian Heg during the years after the Civil War give evidence of both attachment to the new homeland and pride in a Norwegian ethnic identity. Members of ethnic groups who fought in the Civil War undertook the ultimate initiation into American culture and history; they made blood sacrifice to save the Union and preserve American ideals.[1]

LINCOLN AND THE ELECTION OF 1860

The Wisconsin Blue Book devoted an entire issue to commemorating the centennial of the Civil War. In 1860, it asserts, "Wisconsin Republicans . . . had every reason to be eager and optimistic" because "From its beginnings in a little white schoolhouse in Ripon, the Republican flame had spread over Wisconsin like a prairie fire. The billowing smoke in northern skies from Minnesota to Maine proved that Republican fires were burning brightly."

Wisconsin might be viewed as a wellspring of Republican support, but otherwise support for the Republican Party was by no means universal. The prospects for electing a Republican president were nevertheless encouraging. Abraham Lincoln early on appeared as a likely presidential candidate. More than a thousand delegates met in the Springfield, Illinois, statehouse on June 16, 1858, for the Republican State Convention. They chose Lincoln as their candidate for the US Senate, to oppose Democrat Stephen A. Douglas. Senator Douglas, a leading Democrat in Congress, in 1854 had sponsored the Kansas-Nebraska Act, known as popular sovereignty, which Lincoln declared was proslavery or noncommittal. Debating the merits of the act with Douglas in Peoria, Illinois, in October 1854, Lincoln denounced slavery and its extension as a violation of the basic tenets of the Declaration of Independence.

At the convention in June 1858, Lincoln gave his first version of the House Divided speech. "A house divided against itself cannot stand" became the most famous phrase of the senatorial race. "I believe," Lincoln asserted, "this government cannot endure permanently half slave and half free." During the campaign the summer of 1858, the political debates between Lincoln and Douglas became the most famous in American history. The debates moved to cities throughout Illinois, beginning in Ottawa on August 21 and ending in Alton on October 15, 1858.

Douglas accused the Republicans of being abolitionists. Lincoln on the other hand insisted that his House Divided speech was not abolitionist. He intended to resist the further spread of slavery and have new territories kept free. Lincoln considered slavery a moral, social, and political wrong. Yet, as he expressed at the Charleston debate on September 18, "I am not in favor of Negro citizenship." The debates attracted national attention. The reporter for the *New York Times* observed that Lincoln "is clear, concise, logical; his language is eloquent and at perfect command."

Lincoln lost the 1858 Senate election to Douglas. But through his performance he had developed a national reputation, and the Republicans found a new leader in Abraham Lincoln, who was soon being mentioned for the presidency. Lincoln's profile rose in February 1860 when he made a major speech at the Cooper Institute in New York City, saying that the country could afford to let slavery alone where it was, while the Republican votes would prevent it from spreading into the national territories and overrunning the free states. Lincoln's moderate stance on slavery, and on a variety of other divisive issues, was designed to hold the nation together and preserve the Union at whatever cost. Horace Greeley, editor of the *New-York Tribune*, called Lincoln a champion of free labor.

The Republican National Convention, meeting in Chicago on May 18, 1860, nominated Abraham Lincoln for the presidency and Hannibal Hamlin as his running mate. It became a four-way contest.

Lincoln again competed with Stephen Douglas, who in the general election represented the Northern Democrats. Disagreements over the issue of slavery had split the party, and the Southern Democratic Party, a faction of the traditional Democrats, nominated John Breckinridge of Kentucky, an advocate of slavery in the West. Republican breakaways and elements of the former American or Know-Nothing Party formed the Constitutional Union Party and nominated the conservative John Bell of Tennessee.

The Republican Party's platform promised not to interfere with slavery in the states but opposed slavery in the territories. The platform promised a Homestead Act granting free farmland in the West to settler colonists and the funding of a transcontinental railroad. Abolitionists were angry at the selection of a moderate candidate and had little faith in Lincoln. In the general election, Lincoln lost the votes of many abolitionists.

Norwegian Americans responded to and engaged with national politics. In the critical campaign days, *Emigranten*, published in Madison and edited by Carl Fredrik Solberg, was then the only Norwegian-language newspaper published in America. It continued its strong support of the Republican cause. The life story of Colonel Hans Christian Heg—and the history of Norwegian American citizenry as a whole—must be placed in a broad social and political context. Norwegian Americans' response to the presidential election and involvement in public issues are significant aspects of life in the new land. These individuals responded to current events as Norwegian immigrants.

In the forceful article *"Contadini* in Chicago: A Critique of *The Uprooted,"* Rudolph J. Vecoli takes exception to the idea expressed by Oscar Handlin in his influential book *The Uprooted,* written within the assimilationist scholarly tradition. Vecoli fundamentally rejects the notion that immigrants to the United States left their customs behind and sought to assimilate quickly into American society. Instead, Vecoli writes, the Italian *contadini*—peasant farmers—"clung to their traditions and developed strategies to retain their heritage and resist pressures to embrace the American social and economic system."

The mustering of the Fifteenth Wisconsin Regiment, consisting mainly of Norwegian immigrants, supports Vecoli's view of the immigrant experience and adjustment to life in a foreign land. As recruiting began, it became evident that many immigrant citizens of the West wanted to serve, if possible, in regiments of their own countrymen and commanded by officers of their own background, as Theodore C. Blegen describes it. The regiment became a public and national marking of a Norwegian ethnic identity. This sense of identity was evident even before the war: in *Emigranten* for November 12, 1860, Solberg responded jubilantly when the majority of the electoral votes was assured to Lincoln, printing on the front page, "A thousand hurrahs for Lincoln and Hamlin!"

The election was held on Tuesday, November 6, 1860, with a voter turnout of 81.2 percent, the highest in American history up to that time. In the election Lincoln held all of the free states and none of the slave states. He had 180 of the electoral votes, the opposition 123. The split in the Democratic Party elected Lincoln. His election served as the main catalyst of the American Civil War. The Southern states feared a Republican administration would interfere with their internal affairs and slavery. The addition of Minnesota in 1858 and Oregon in 1859 as free states furthermore assured complete control of the federal government by free-state, antislavery politicians. In 1804 New Jersey became the last Northern state to commit to abolition. Many of the Republican Party's members were abolitionists and more extreme than the new president. Lincoln's election triggered cries for disunion across the slaveholding South.

South Carolina became the first state to secede from the federal Union on December 20, 1860. By February 1, 1861, six more states had seceded, all in the Lower South region of the United States: Mississippi, Florida, Alabama, Georgia, Louisiana, and Texas. Delegates from the seven slave states convened in Montgomery, Alabama, on February 4, 1861, and adopted a Confederate Constitution and founded the Confederate States of America; the new government quickly formed its own Confederate States Army. The Civil War began on April 12, 1861, with Confederate forces firing on Fort Sumter, a Union fort in Charleston harbor, South Carolina. After the outbreak of hostilities, four slave states of the Upper South also seceded and joined the Confederacy: Arkansas, Tennessee, North Carolina, and Virginia. During the fall of 1861, the Confederacy suffered secession "in the mountains of western Virginia," which became the free state of West Virginia. The Confederate Congress later admitted the slave states of Missouri and Kentucky as members of the Confederacy, even though neither state had seceded from the Union. No foreign government ever recognized the Confederacy as an independent nation. During the Civil War, the loyal states became known as the Union.[2]

THE SLAVE SOCIETY OF THE SOUTH

Hans Christian Heg's aversion to slavery might derive from his early years in Norway and the values of a Haugean upbringing, and later growing to adulthood in Wisconsin with its unrivaled antislavery strategy. This conviction stayed with Heg until he fell at the battle of Chickamauga.

The first chapter in Fergus Bordewich's *Bound for Canaan* is titled "An Evil Without Remedy." Bordewich introduces the chapter on slavery by reflecting on the memories of an individual victim, in this case on the personal experience of Josiah Henson, born into slavery on June 15, 1789, on the eastern shore of Chesapeake Bay, Maryland, on a farm belonging to Francis Newman, whose property Henson's father was. His mother was the property of a neighbor. Josiah's earliest memory was the day his father came home with his ear cut off. Josiah was five or six years old when this horrifying event occurred, likely in 1795. Many years later, as he himself tells the story, he recalled how his father appeared one day covered in blood and in a state of great excitement. His head was bloody and his back lacerated. Enslaved people from surrounding plantations were ordered to witness his punishment for their "moral improvement."

Josiah's father's offense was to physically protect Josiah's mother— then hired out to Newman—who was being brutally assaulted by Newman's overseer, who very likely intended to rape her. The punishment of an enslaved person for lifting his hand on a white man's body, which was seen as rebellion, was sometimes execution or occasionally castration. One hundred lashes were laid on Josiah's father by a local blacksmith, fifty lashes at a time. Bleeding and faint, he was held up against the whipping post and his right ear fastened to it with a tack. The blacksmith then sliced off the ear with a knife. Josiah relates how the brutal degradation caused his father to become a different man, brooding and morose and considered intractable, as slave owners typically described human property that no longer responded compliantly to command. As a consequence, Josiah said, "off he was sent to Alabama. What was his after fate neither my mother nor I ever learned."

In due course, all the remaining Hensons—Josiah's three sisters, two brothers, his mother, and himself—were put up at auction. Enslaved people from other farms were frantic at being sold away from Maryland to the Deep South, with its reputation of brutal treatment of enslaved people. Human suffering and human cruelty were both evident at slave auctions, which separated parents and children, husbands and wives, and lifelong friends from each other. The account based on Josiah's reflections of the auction, which took place when he was still a child, includes the following: "The memory of this event remained engraved in Josiah's memory until the end of his life: the huddled group of anxious slaves, the crowd of bidders, the clinical examining of muscles and teeth, his mother's raw fear. His brothers and sisters were bid off one by one, while his mother, holding his hand, looked on in 'an agony of grief,' whose meaning only slowly dawned on the little boy as the sale proceeded."

His mother was sold to a farmer in Montgomery County, close to the new national capital Washington. Young Josiah was bought by a

Auction of enslaved people in Montgomery, Alabama. Alabama Department of Archives and History

man who kept a tavern at the site of Rockville, then just a country crossroad, where Josiah was taken and, as he recalls, "put . . . into his negro quarters with about forty others . . . all strangers to me." Josiah felt brutalized and degraded, and received no sympathy. "I soon fell sick," he relates, "and lay for some days almost dead on the ground."

Similar inhumane treatments of enslaved people and indifference to their existence as members of the human race persisted, and were well known to Hans Christian Heg and others. The story of Josiah Henson and his family gives insight into the dire circumstances that triggered antislavery and abolitionist sentiments. The slave state Maryland, being a border state, did not leave the Union during the Civil War. In the book *How the Word Is Passed*, Clint Smith gives a revealing contemporary portrait of America as a slave-owning nation. The legacy of the Civil War remains much in evidence; one reviewer commends Smith for skillfully documenting how enslavement echoes everywhere and sees his contribution as needed reckoning.

The reality of American slavery was, as shown above, often brutal, barbaric, and violent. The myth of Black people's racial inferiority nevertheless developed and persisted as a common justification for continuing the system. White slaveholders—slavery advocates claimed—were performing an act of kindness by exposing the Black people they held as human property to discipline, hard work, and morality. After the transatlantic slave trade was outlawed by Congress in 1808, a domestic slave trade became commonplace across the South. Due to a booming cotton industry, an estimated one million enslaved people were forcibly transferred from the Upper South to the Lower South between 1810 and 1860. By 1830 one million people labored in the cultivation of cotton, and almost all of them were enslaved. Cotton constituted more than half of the global export of the

Enslaved people receiving cotton bales on board a steamer for further transportation. Alabama Department of Archives and History

United States. In 1861 when Alabama seceded from the Union to join the Confederacy, 45 percent of the state's total population was enslaved Black people.

Slavery was interwoven into the South's predominately agrarian economy, as well as into its political and cultural life, even though only a relatively small portion of the population actually owned enslaved people. The enslaved must not be viewed simply as passive victims, however. Many resisted the foundation of slavery; many ran away or even took part in uprisings and confrontational rebellions— for example, the bloody Nat Turner insurrection in Virginia in 1831, cited earlier. On the eve of the Civil War, nearly four million Africans and their descendants toiled as enslaved laborers.[3]

ETHNIC REGIMENTS

Melting Pot Soldiers by William Burton provides an overview of the formation of German, Irish, Scandinavian, Scottish, French, as well as multiethnic regiments in the North during the Civil War and the social and political situation that fostered them. The 1860 census counted some 34 million residents of the United States. Thirteen percent of American residents were foreign-born, numbering well over four million people, almost half residing in the New England and mid-Atlantic states. Most of the remainder lived in the states of the Old Northwest. Less than ten percent of the nation's immigrant population lived in the South.

Considering Civil War ethnic engagement broadly places the Norwegian American participation in a valid historical context. Carl Schurz gave impetus to the formation of ethnic military companies and regiments. German-born Schurz, along with many other German Forty-Eighters—Europeans who took part in the revolutions of 1848—moved to America. In 1854 he settled in Watertown, Wisconsin, where he gained admittance to practice law. He was dedicated to the newly established Republican Party, which Forty-Eighters supported because of its antislavery stance. A greatly influential ethnic politician, Schurz became the major German American orator for Lincoln's 1860 election campaign and swung many German voters into the Republican Party. After Fort Sumter, he contacted President Lincoln, US senators, and state officials in an effort to establish an ethnic presence in the army. Schurz persisted in advising Lincoln on how to run the war and what to do for German Americans.

Prominent German American leaders in Chicago, as elsewhere, promoted the idea of an all-German regiment. The result was the Illinois Twenty-Fourth Infantry. The Illinois story was repeated in every Northern state where ethnic numbers and leaders supported the effort. German leaders agitated for German regiments from the beginning of the war. Much ethnic recruiting was undertaken in languages other than English, but the appeals were exactly the same as those for all Americans: "The Union was threatened and patriots should join up and fight to defend that Union."

Only the Germans and the Irish in Illinois organized regiments in that state; the Scottish effort there failed, but the Scots succeeded in New York with the Seventy-Ninth Militia Regiment. Burton details the impressive number of Irish and German regiments. He describes New York as the largest Irish city in the world; nearly half of its 800,000 residents were foreign-born, and the Irish the largest number of those by far. An Irish regiment, the Sixty-Ninth New York Volunteer Militia, already existed when the Civil War began. As the "Fighting Sixty-Ninth" it became the best-known militia unit in the country. Many German military units existed: Ohio had six German regiments, and Pennsylvania had five. Wisconsin contributed one German militia regiment. The regiments served for a period of three years. Ethnic regiments appeared throughout the states of the North.

Other ethnic populations instituted separate military units as well. They might initially organize in companies that merged to form a regiment. In New York French immigrants formed the Fifty-Third New York Infantry. There were Hungarian and Spanish legions that became companies. The effort to form an Italian regiment called Garibaldi Guard ended up with Hungarian, Spanish, Italian, French, and German recruits. In May 1861 the Garibaldi Guard, the Thirty-Ninth New York Infantry, succeeded in filling up ten companies, each with a separate ethnic identity. Many groups thus served the Union within their ethnic identity in a multitude of ways, yet the great majority of ethnic recruits served in regular American military organizations.[4]

Norwegians in the Civil War

In 1860 in the states of the Upper Midwest—Illinois, Wisconsin, Iowa, and Minnesota—were about fifty-five thousand people of Norwegian birth or ancestry. In the other regions of the United States there were perhaps a thousand Norwegians. The Norwegians in the Midwest consisted mostly of families; there were few single adults, and a large percentage of the children had been born in America.

The exact number of Norwegian-born soldiers in the Civil War Union Army may never be known, but based on available data Jerry Rosholt asserts that they numbered 6,500. Some American-born Norwegians may also have been included. My own research shows an increasing sense of solidarity among all Norwegians in America, and an emerging Norwegian American identity. In 1847 Ole Munch Ræder, then in America with Norwegian state support to study various jury systems, wrote "Our people in America . . . already act in unity and are thereby protected against foreign influence, since the internal relationship among them is stronger than between them and other people who live here." The new Norwegian American identity may at least in part be accepted as the self-assertion of an immigrant people toward the homeland. In this respect Norwegians acted like most colonists.

Petter Drevland, in his thesis on reasons for Norwegians to enlist in the Civil War, cites Orm Øverland's theory of homemaking myths, which function to claim the United States as the rightful home of many immigrant groups. In the Norwegian case, the mythic figure Leif Erikson and his claimed early discovery give Norwegian Americans a special and natural right to a home in the United States.

Initially the Lincoln administration relied entirely on volunteers to fill the ranks; patriotic emotions were fortified by large, tempting bounties. Eventually, however, conscription was required after enlistment had slowed. The Enrollment Act of 1863 was enacted March 3; it required the enrollment of every male citizen and those immigrants who had filed for citizenship if between the ages of twenty and forty-five. Quotas were assigned in each state and each congressional district, with deficiencies in volunteers to be met by conscription. If a district failed to reach the quota of volunteers, a draft lottery was initiated. Not only Norwegians but immigrants of all nationalities volunteered or were drafted in numbers that more than equaled their percentage of the population. There were more of them in the prescribed age for military service.

Drevland employed the America letters, correspondence back home, as his main sources. His qualified study of the letters found four main reasons given by enlistees: ideological, economical, religious, and a sense of duty. He examines and analyzes the reasons in a logical fashion. While this study does not expand on each reason given, Drevland's work shows that they all deserve consideration.

Like American-born citizens, Norwegians and other immigrant populations fought the Civil War for various reasons; many were motivated by an ideological opposition to slavery, others by loyalty to their adopted homeland, and still others sought economic opportunity. In the introduction to Waldemar Ager's *Chickamauga: Colonel Heg and His Boys*, Harry Cleven quotes Bersven Nelson, a young recruit in the Fifteenth Wisconsin, who gives some of his reasons for enlistment. He had immigrated from the Målselv valley of Finnmark only a few months earlier. The hundred-dollar bounty, thirteen dollars a month wages, and free food and clothing seemed a great windfall to him. Motives might be mixed. In a history of Norwegian participation in the Civil War, Karl Jakob Skarstein considers the political incentive. Politicians might use their ethnic background to gain support among immigrants by mustering an ethnic military unit and thus draw attention to their candidacy. Skarstein further describes the motive of linguistic security for organizing an ethnic division among the many immigrants who had not mastered English and would feel safer on the battlefield by having officers who spoke their language. The enlisted Norwegian immigrants showed great patriotism to their new homeland. Yet names like "St. Olaf's Rifles" and "Odin's Rifles," two companies in the Fifteenth Wisconsin, show a deduced Viking warrior ancestry. The adjutant general of the US Army in connection with the presentation of a status report added the following words, "All hail, Norsemen, descendants of the Vikings, let your hordes, as in days of old, sweep down upon the South, crushing as with Tor's hammer the Southerner who meets you on the field of battle."

At the time of the war's outbreak, the state of Minnesota was barely three years old. The decennial census in 1860 captured 172,023 residents. Its population grew rapidly thereafter, but nevertheless Minnesota was sparsely populated in the enormous area that constituted the state. It was a young and remarkably diverse population. The census in 1860 showed that more than 65 percent of all Minnesotans were native-born whites. European immigration to Minnesota climbed steadily in the territorial decade: "By 1860 Scandinavians and Irish each made up 7 percent of the population, and one out of ten Minnesotans was German-born." By 1870, however, the Scandinavians had overtaken the Germans to become the largest foreign-born element in Minnesota's population. Within the Scandinavian group Norwegians were the most numerous. During the decade dominated by the Civil War, Norwegians settled throughout the state. Statistics from their military service in the Union forces show where they settled and in what strength. Single men outnumbered women, a typical situation in all nineteenth-century frontier communities.

As noted by Brian Horrigan, at the eruption of the Civil War in April 1861, "young Minnesota men headed off to fight in staggering numbers—one of the highest per capita rates of enlistment in the Union." The First Minnesota Volunteer Infantry Regiment played a pivotal role in many battles and holds a special place in the history of Minnesota. Minnesota's governor, Alexander Ramsey, was in Washington, DC, when the Civil War commenced on April 12, 1861, and he immediately promised President Lincoln a regiment of a thousand volunteer soldiers from Minnesota. It was the first body of troops raised by the state for Civil War service, and it was among the first regiments of any state offered for national service. The First Minnesota mustered for duty at Fort Snelling on April 29, 1861. There were fifty-three Norwegian-born volunteer recruits. The legendary First Minnesota won a reputation as a hard-fighting regiment and became a symbol of the Civil War service of all Minnesotans. Its dramatic action at the Battle of Gettysburg came the summer of 1863, when on the second day of fighting, July 2, it helped General Winfield S. Hancock hold the Union line against advancing Confederate soldiers. The next day the Minnesota First—with a great sacrificial loss of lives—along with other Union troops repulsed twelve thousand Confederates—including three brigades of Virginians under General George E. Pickett. There were only half that many Union troops; the action effectively ended the Battle of Gettysburg and served as a turning point in the Civil War. The First Minnesota Volunteer Infantry Regiment has three monuments in its honor at Gettysburg.

More than twelve hundred Norwegian-born Minnesotans enlisted in the Civil War, in one of the state's eleven infantry regiments or other military units. Minnesota contributed men for service in the Union armies from all ranks of life, the majority volunteers. In the September 16, 1861, issue, *Emigranten* carried an advertisement by Lars K. Aaker of Goodhue County appealing for Norwegian volunteers to form two or three companies. In its endorsement, the paper assumed that Minnesota would soon count "as many alert and un-afraid Norwegians as needed so that the companies' ranks can be filled within a short time." Aaker, an immigrant from Telemark, had a fine career in state politics. Goodhue County had considerable colonies of Swedish and Norwegian settlers. The appeal apparently attracted a sufficient number of volunteers for at least one company. Hans Mattson in his reminiscences takes credit for raising Company D, consisting of Swedes and Norwegians, where he served as captain. Lars Aaker served as first lieutenant.

Mattson was born in Skåne, Sweden, and immigrated to the United States in 1851. In August 1853 he led a group of several hundred Swedish immigrants to Goodhue County and formed a settlement soon known as Vasa. The Third Minnesota Volunteer Infantry Regiment was mustered by companies, among these Company D, at Fort Snelling in October and November of 1861. Mattson, who during his lifetime was one of the best-known Swedish American politicians, explains the situation: "Although Company D was the only military organization in our state consisting exclusively of Scandinavians, there were quite a number of those nationalities in every regiment and company organized afterwards."[5]

THE FIFTEENTH WISCONSIN REGIMENT

In 1860 most of Wisconsin's 775,000 people lived along Lake Michigan and in the southern counties. A little more than a third of the people living in the state were foreign-born. Of these, 44 percent were from the German states. As many as twenty German-language newspapers were published in Wisconsin in 1860, demonstrating German weight and standing in state affairs. The Irish constituted the second-largest group after the German settlers. Norway also provided a large number of immigrants: in 1860 there were 29,557 Norwegian-born settlers in the state of Wisconsin.

News of the firing on Fort Sumter reached Wisconsin on April 13, 1861. According to the *Weekly Telegraph*, published in Kenosha, it created an excitement "never equaled," with the consensus that "treason and rebellion must be crushed at once." News of the defeat of federal troops at the Battle of Bull Run on July 21 represented a serious setback for the North, adding greatly to the anguish that already existed. President Lincoln's call for military volunteers met with an exhilarating response throughout the North. In April 1861 Wisconsin was asked to provide one regiment. Governor Alexander Randall issued a proclamation offering "opportunities" to all existing militia companies for enlistment; within ten days Randall had enough volunteers for five regiments. The First Wisconsin Voluntary Regiment, organized in 1861, consisted of ten militia companies. On August 20, 1861, the War Department called for five additional Wisconsin regiments. Governor Randall officially requested that one of these be composed of Germans, and the Ninth Wisconsin was organized as a German immigrant regiment. The Eleventh Wisconsin was for the most part Irish. Wisconsin furnished fifty-two regiments as well as four regiments and one company of cavalry, twelve batteries of light artillery, one regiment of heavy artillery, one company of sharpshooters, and two brigade bands—the latter marched while playing military music. The recorded 91,379 Wisconsin recruits, of which 79,934 were volunteers, showed, as the 1962 *Blue Book* claims, great patriotism in Wisconsin, proven even more when 1,263 extra men over all calls were furnished.

Emigranten for August 26, 1861, printed, in Norwegian translation, Randall's description of how the infantry regiments would be organized as well as that one regiment would be German: "Each regiment will consist of ten companies, and each company will consist of no fewer than 83 and no more than 101 men. The fewest number of men in a regiment would thus be 830 and the largest 1010 men."[6]

The Fifteenth Organized

Blegen suggests that Governor Randall's promotion of a German regiment was likely what influenced John A. Johnson to open a roll call on August 31 for recruiting a Scandinavian company, calling for at least eighty-three men. On September 2, 1861, *Emigranten* published Johnson's proposal and strongly endorsed it: "It cannot fail that there must be many countrymen among us who feel warmly enough for our new fatherland to dare a combat in order to preserve the Union and make it possible for the government to exert the laws constitutionally over the entire country." Two weeks later, on September 16, *Emigranten* reported an enthusiastic response to Johnson's call. The company would have Madison as its meeting place (*Samlingssted*).

The biography of John A. Johnson, written by Agnes M. Larson, gives deep insight into Johnson's life and career. Born in Telemark, Norway, he in 1844, when twelve years old, came to Wisconsin together with his family. He is described as "an alert, sensitive, gentle lad." The Johnsons first settled at Heart Prairie, where Claus Clausen served as pastor in the small church built on the shores of Whitewater Lake. Clausen, and the newspaper he edited, *Emigranten*, strengthened the family's concerns about slavery. In 1852 the Johnsons moved to Koshkonong, where John A. Johnson in 1854 purchased about 140 acres of land. Larson describes throughout the biography Johnson's great success in business and in politics.

At the end of the Civil War, John A. Johnson compiled a detailed 160-page history of the Fifteenth Wisconsin Regiment. Most of the section on the history of the regiment was composed by his younger brother Colonel Ole C. Johnson, who played an important part in the regiment's wartime command. There were several contributors, noted Knud Langeland, including Chaplain Claus Clausen, who "added his observations on moral and religious phases of military

Ole C. Johnson served as captain of Company B, and later succeeded Hans C. Heg as colonel of the Fifteenth Wisconsin Regiment. Wisconsin Historical Society

life as experienced by men of the regiment." Many of the brief biographies are by John Johnson's own hand. Larson describes it as both a factual account and a subjective document.

Hans C. Heg and John A. Johnson had early on considered organizing a Norwegian regiment. Heg informed Johnson that he intended to go to war. His May proposal to have convict labor at Waupun make uniforms gave strong evidence of his support of a Scandinavian regiment. He had also handed in his resignation as prison commissioner, which Governor Randall refused to accept. On September 25, Heg was renominated with acclaim by the state convention. But *Emigranten* for October 14, 1861, printed Heg's letter, dated October 3, to the chair of the convention in which he declined the nomination, adding, "With complete confidence that the committee, whose fore-man you are, will fill my position with a liberal, courageous, and humane man, I give you my assurance that I of my whole heart will support his selection."

On September 25, 1861, a committee of prominent Norwegians, including Heg and Johnson, who took the lead, met at the state cap-itol in Madison. They adopted a formal resolution to raise a regiment. *Emigranten*, on September 30, appealed for support from the Nor-wegian community and predicted great success. A letter, signed by among others J. A. Johnson and C. F. Solberg, *Emigranten*'s editor, to inform Governor Randall of the resolution to raise a "Scandinavian Brigade . . . for the war now pending in this our adopted Country," recommended that Hans C. Heg be appointed as colonel and Kiler K. Jones as lieutenant colonel. The project had Governor Randall's full and immediate support, and on October 1, 1861, he endorsed the committee's proposal and offered Hans C. Heg the commission of colonel of the new regiment. It was then officially designated the Fifteenth Wisconsin.

Emigranten, on October 7, stated editorially that it does not quite know how to sufficiently congratulate the coming regiment with its colonel. The editorial praises Heg's personal qualifications:

> Young, energetic and courageous, proud and solidly honest, to a high degree considerate of the welfare of his subordinates, with an excel-lent amount of practical sound sense, and with the increased familiar-ity with men and things which his work as state official has given him, he will be the best man we know in America to be at the head of such an undertaking. Our countrymen can gather around him as their chief with unqualified trust. They will neither have to complain about their treatment as soldiers nor need to fear that the Norwegian name's honor will not be in good hands.

The Fifteenth Wisconsin was the only all-Scandinavian, mainly Norwegian, regiment in the war on either side, the Union or the Confederacy. Its roster of field officers and staff with remarks is a guide into the regiment's administration. Kiler K. Jones served as lieutenant general, but already in March 1862 his service was revoked by order. Ole C. Johnson, following his brief venture as captain of Company B, rose successively to be major, lieutenant colonel, and in Chickamauga colonel. Heg's brother, Ole Heg, had the rank of quartermaster and served from October 28, 1861, to June 6, 1862.

At Colonel Heg's recommendation, Governor Randall commissioned the Reverend Claus L. Clausen as the Fifteenth's chaplain. Chaplain Clausen was very popular with the regiment's soldiers; in his honor the men of Company K named themselves Clausen's Guards. Stephen Oliver Himoe immigrated to America in 1846 and was a graduate of St. Louis Medical School. In July 1857 he married Colonel Heg's sister Andrea Heg and became a member of the Heg family. Colonel Heg recommended Governor Randall appoint Dr. Himoe surgeon (*Feltlæge*) of the Fifteenth.

The Norwegian composition of the Fifteenth Wisconsin becomes apparent in the names of the ten companies that were mustered, each led by a captain. The captains listed are the first ones mustered, and only in a few cases will the names of later captains be given here.

Company A. St. Olaf's Rifles was predominantly from the city of Chicago and the men were mainly recruited by Kiler Jones. Men from Boone County, Illinois, were also recruited. Captain Andrew Thorkildson.

Company B. Wergeland's Guards was made up largely of volunteers from the area of Koshkonong in Jefferson County and from Dane County. Captain Ole C. Johnson, Captain Ole Ramussen Dahl.

Company C. Norway Bear Hunters was mainly recruited from the city of Milwaukee and Racine County. Captain Frederik R. Berg.

Company D. Norway Wolf Hunters (aka Waupun Company) was recruited from a number of counties and from Waupun in Dodge County. Captain Charles Campbell, later Captain Albert Skofstad.

Company E. Odin's Rifles had a few recruits from Nicollet and Fillmore Counties in Minnesota and many men from Dane County, Wisconsin. Captain John Ingmundson.

Company F. K. K.'s Protectors (aka Valdres Company) mainly recruited in Manitowoc and Door Counties. Captain Charles Gustavson.

Company G. Rock River Rangers was mainly recruited from Blue Mounds in Dane County, and from Primrose and Rock Counties, Wisconsin. Captain John A. Gordon.

Company H. Heg's Rifles (aka Voss Company) had some recruits from towns like Decorah in Iowa and also some from Minnesota. Captain Knud J. Sime.

Company I. Scandinavian Mountaineers (aka Waupaca Company) had recruits from Waupaca County, and other towns and counties in Wisconsin. There were also recruits from Chicago and a few from Minnesota. Captain August Gasman.

Company K. Clausen's Guards had predominately recruits from Freeborn County, Minnesota, and Winneshiek County, Iowa. Captain Mons Grinager.

Emigranten, on December 23, 1861, noted, "The other day the recruiting lieutenants O. Solberg and O. P. Slette returned from Iowa and Minnesota with 40 recruits for Company K, the 10th in the Regiment, which has its name 'Clausen's Guards,' from the army chaplain."

The ten companies illustrate the Fifteenth Wisconsin's extensive geographic representation.[7]

Recruitment

Recruiting broadly, the Fifteenth Wisconsin may be described as a regiment of the old Northwest, the common contemporary designation for the states in the Upper Midwest. Recruiting officers were chosen and began their work in Norwegian settlements immediately. Blegen assesses this enlistment effort: "Men of Scandinavian blood joined the colors with enthusiasm in Wisconsin, Minnesota, Iowa, Illinois, and other states in which they had but recently settled." Fifteenth Wisconsin recruiters sought volunteers in these states. Governor Randall called Ole C. Johnson, fresh out of Beloit College, to serve as recruiting officer for the Fifteenth. He was well qualified and mastered both English and Norwegian. Unfortunately, he found recruiting a disagreeable task. His experience as a recruiter was likely not unique, and might be a clarifying amendment to Blegen's strongly positive judgment. Johnson met human nature and found that not all the men he talked to could feel the patriotic call to leave home and risk their lives. Ole Johnson abandoned his attempt at recruiting and shortly thereafter became captain of Company B.

Hans Christian Heg, as colonel, devoted himself tirelessly to securing a robust response to the drive for volunteers. The Madison newspaper *Emigranten* became his main avenue to make calls to enlist. This Norwegian American organ gave much space to the proposed regiment and the Northern cause. As noted earlier, its September 30 issue advocated the unique opportunity the regiment gave the Scandinavians of the West to enter the army. The editorial even appealed to an ethnic competitive spirit and made an issue of the German and Irish regiments being mustered. The Scandinavians could clearly not allow themselves to be outmatched.

The campaign to organize the Fifteenth Wisconsin received effective aid from both English and Norwegian newspapers. Solberg published a special number of *Emigranten* composed of articles dealing broadly with the Fifteenth Wisconsin and the Civil War and circulated this particular issue widely as an aid to recruiting. Colonel Heg persisted throughout the autumn months in writing calls that were broadcast in the states of the Upper Midwest. *Emigranten* for October 7, 1861, published an appeal directed not only to Norwegians but also to Swedes and Danes. Heg asked for a thousand men.

Colonel Heg reassured potential volunteers that the officers of the regiment spoke the Scandinavian languages, which would afford an opportunity to enter the service for Scandinavian men who did not yet speak English. Heg reminded them that "The government of our adopted country is in danger."

In *Emigranten* on November 18, 1861, Heg penned an emotional article titled "To the Scandinavians in Wisconsin." His question: "Should we Scandinavians sit still and watch that our American, German, and English-born fellow citizens fight for us without helping them?" The Fifteenth Wisconsin was not yet full and could not be mobilized before it had at least nine hundred men. "It is assumed [*antages*]," Heg continued, "only 600 men have been enlisted." Heg concluded by making a fervent appeal: "Come, then, young Norsemen and take part in defending the country's cause, and fulfill an urgent duty, which everyone who is able to owes the country in which he lives. Let us join together and deliver untarnished to posterity the old honorable Norwegian name." In his recruitment propaganda, Heg invokes his fellow Norwegians and their heroic values rather than being a spokesman for Uncle Sam.

Despite Heg's complaint, the recruiting and organization of the Fifteenth Wisconsin went rapidly under his supervision. In December 1861 the regiment was assembled at Camp Randall, Madison, ready to be mobilized.[8]

THE FIFTEENTH WISCONSIN MOBILIZED

Colonel Heg conducted a warm and regular exchange of letters with his wife, Gunild. On February 11, 1862, he wrote about the Fifteenth Wisconsin from its headquarters at Camp Randall: "We have in all 810 privates and about 40 officers, our Regiment is now full to the 850 men and I shall probably be mustered into United States service." The letter evidences a close relationship through Heg's concern for his family's welfare and his detailed instruction as to how Gunild and the children—unless they were not well and the weather was not good—could visit him in Madison.

Colonel Heg took command of the Fifteenth Wisconsin on January 15, 1862. On February 17, 1862, *Emigranten* announced: "The Norwegian Regiment (*Det norske Regiment*) is now full, up to the minimum number, and its commanding officer Colonel Heg was Thursday sworn into the service of the United States." Identifying the regiment as Norwegian, not Scandinavian, was an important distinction. The soldiers were all Norwegian except for about thirty men: three Swedes, three Danes, three Irish, and several officers, surgeons, and medical staffers. Blegen emphasizes the regiment's Norwegian composition by pointing out that it contained no fewer than 128 men whose first name was Ole.

In the afternoon the soldiers met at Camp Randall and formed a large square. In the open middle of the square stood Colonel Heg, the regiment's officers, and a Captain Lamot, chief for Wisconsin in enrolling soldiers. Captain Lamot read the oath, and the regiment's soldiers, their right arms held high, swore loyalty to the United States, to the president, and to all military officers. In a brief speech to the regiment following the swearing in, Heg reminded the soldiers that "they represented the entire Norwegian population and must under all circumstances conduct themselves in a manner that made them and the old Norwegian name worthy." He concluded by promising to do everything in his power to deserve their confidence, calling for them to stand together "through thick and thin" (*last og brast*). After a "long live" greeting to Colonel Heg and a three-times-three hurrah by the soldiers, the ceremony ended, and the regiment marched to Madison and paraded along the streets. It was the first time the regiment visited the city, and the march attracted a large crowd of people. The *Wisconsin State Journal*, published in Madison, remarked: "This attractive Regiment marched through the city this afternoon and performed its maneuvers with great precision."

There were at that time about three thousand men at Camp Randall. Two regiments in addition to the Fifteenth Wisconsin were also in the process of organization. Over 3,600 Norwegians enlisted in various Wisconsin regiments, including the Fifteenth. Arriving at Camp Randall in December the previous year, the prospective soldiers in the Fifteenth had their first taste of military life. Their experiences were typical of all Wisconsin military units that were getting ready for service in the South. Much of the time was devoted to drill.

Camp Randall had a negative reputation. Ben (Bersven) Nelson of Company I, the Scandinavian Mountaineers, described the conditions at the camp. The sleeping quarters and the dining hall were both built of plain boards. There was a large stove, but it did not help much against the severe cold during the winter of 1862. The dining hall had ten tables, each large enough to accommodate one hundred men. There were no chairs, so the men had to stand as they ate. The food was not of the best quality, Nelson complained: "We had to eat what was dished out or else starve."

The Fifteenth Wisconsin, along with two other regiments, was ready to depart for the front on March 2, 1862. Ben Nelson related how they left Camp Randall early in the morning in a blinding snowstorm and marched to the railroad station: "A vast number of Norwegians were gathered at the station to say farewell to husbands, sons, brothers, and sweethearts; when the train left, there was waving of hats and handkerchiefs—as one might expect."

Emigranten's publisher Carl Fredrik Solberg accompanied the Wisconsin Fifteenth to Missouri as a correspondent of his own newspaper, and in the number dated March 17, 1862, he shared a long segment on the regiment's departure for the South. The Fifteenth Wisconsin upon its arrival in Chicago on its way to Missouri was met by members of the Norwegian Nora Society. The Nora Society was formed on July 18, 1860, as a purely Norwegian society, thus

"For Gud og Vort Land" (For God and Our Country). The Nora Society presented the men in the Fifteenth Wisconsin Regiment with this banner. Vesterheim Norwegian-American Museum

showing the limits of pan-Scandinavian sentiment. There was a competitive national spirit with the Swedish Svea Society and the Danish Dania Society, both founded earlier. Nora was a men's society, heavily involved in the Norwegian war effort, and gave evidence of Norwegian American social, cultural, and political interests outside the church. It displayed a remarkable aristocratic strain and sought inspiration from the heroic age of Norway's patron saint, St. Olaf. The company of the Fifteenth Wisconsin the St. Olaf Rifles, formed in Chicago, evinced the Nora Society's strong identification with an exalted past.

The Nora Society entertained the men in the regiment and presented them with a banner, paid for through subscription, with the American colors on one side and on the reverse the American and Norwegian arms united, the Norwegian being a picture of a lion with an ax on a red field. The banner bore the inscription "For Gud og Vort Land" (For God and Our Country). The regiment then departed for St. Louis, and Solberg reported the following: "When the regiment went south, I went with it to St. Louis and spent a while in the camp and field, sending home letters to my paper concerning the regiment and military history generally." The soldiers of the Fifteenth Wisconsin Regiment were prepared for battle.[9]

CHAPTER 5

Service in the American Civil War

THE BROTHERS' WAR

Calling any civil war a brothers' war is justified when fellow citizens of a united nation take up arms against each other, but the hostilities of the 1860s between North and South in the relatively young independent democracy went deeper than state boundaries. There were examples of the insurrection placing family members on opposing sides of the deadly discord—father against son, sibling against sibling. It became a tragic legacy of the war.

The Civil War itself, with its violent fighting and battles at close quarters, caused tremendous loss of human life in both the Northern and the Southern forces. Waldemar Ager recorded 67,058 battlefield casualties in the Northern troops; 43,012 died of wounds. There were in addition 224,586 men who died because of sickness and 24,872 as a result of accidents or other causes. A total of 359,528 men from the Northern states gave their lives in this bloody war. Many of the 275,175 wounded soldiers remained crippled for life.

Losses in the Confederate forces also amounted to about a quarter million men; nearly 100,000 fell on the field of battle or died because of their wounds. The loss of lives in the North and the South combined amounted to more than 600,000 men. Looking at casualties in individual battles might more overtly bring to mind the horrors of the war. Consider the Battle of Shiloh, to which Harry Hansen devotes an entire chapter in *The Civil War*. For two days, April 6–7, 1862, Confederate forces and the Union Army engaged in a brutal battle in Shiloh, thirty miles north of Corinth in southwestern Tennessee. The result was a massive carnage impossible to visualize or comprehend. In the seminal military campaign study *This Terrible Sound*, Peter Cozzens references both the Union and the Confederate sides and focuses on individual historical figures. He offers the following example from Kentucky, a border state: Colonel Joseph Horace Lewis of the Sixth Kentucky brigade at Shiloh had three horses shot out from under him while leading his regiment. He would engage in battles at both Stones River and Chickamauga. Historians have described the battle at Shiloh as notable in terms of the Union troops' inexperience a year after the war had begun and "the ease with which the whole Union war machine was thrown into confusion by a surprise attack." Wisconsin infantry regiments, the Sixteenth and the Eighteenth, together lost more than 450 men killed or wounded. In the classic volume *The Civil War and Reconstruction* appears the following assessment: "Shiloh passed into history, to be refought endlessly in post-mortem reviews and divisional reunions. On both sides losses were heavy, with Confederate casualties numbering 10,699 and those of the Union 13,047, more wounded and killed in two days than Americans had lost in the Revolution, the War of 1812, and the Mexican War combined."[1]

THE CIVIL WAR AND THE FIFTEENTH

From the regiment's departure for St. Louis on March 2, 1862, until near the end of the Civil War in April 1865, when its surviving soldiers were mustered out—companies A, B, and E on December 1, 1864, and the other companies in January and February—the Fifteenth

Wisconsin participated in a total of twenty-six battles and skirmishes as a part of the Union forces operations in Missouri, Kentucky, Mississippi, Tennessee, Alabama, and Georgia. Some of the most important engagements in the regiment's history are Island Number Ten, Perryville, Stones River, Chickamauga, Chattanooga (Missionary Ridge), Resaca, New Hope Church, and Kennesaw Mountain. Some of these important landmarks will be considered from a broad historical point of view. They document the leadership of Colonel Hans Christian Heg, and following his death at Chickamauga that of his successors. Theodore C. Blegen notes that the history of the Fifteenth Wisconsin "and the biography of Colonel Heg are merged from the spring day when the train carrying the immigrant soldiers out of the Wisconsin capital until the battle of Chickamauga, a year and a half later."

History is the study of change over time. During three years among the Union forces, the Fifteenth Wisconsin was progressively transformed from its initial mustering by the demands of its wartime mission. Its members experienced grueling campaigns, bloody battles, great loss of fellow soldiers, new recruitments, field and camp life, and separation from family. Correspondence back home relates the men's experience, thoughts, and emotions. Harry Cleven makes the important point that many of the men did not return to their homes or live to tell about their experience. During the Civil War the Fifteenth Wisconsin lost by death nearly a third of its original enrollment.

Heg's own correspondence, the majority family letters to Gunild and their children, especially to Edmund, the oldest son, and occasionally to his younger daughter, Hilda, will regularly be cited throughout the present chapter. The youngest, Elmer Heg, born in 1861, is a regular subject in Heg's correspondence. On October 23, 1862, in a letter to Gunild, Heg expresses his longing to "take a trip home . . .

long enough to see you all, and especially to see that little rat Elmer that you write so much about." Heg regularly refers to Elmer as Nebby. In a letter dated July 3, 1863, Heg wrote: "You may tell my little Rat—Nebby—that I am shooting the Rebels for him now." In a letter to daughter Hilda dated July 9, 1863, Heg expresses his wish that "I want my girl to be one of the nicest and smartest little Lady to be found," and then refers to Elmer: "I hear that Nebby is such a hard little case—I shall have to make an officer of him."

The correspondence represents a major source and a personal account of Heg's military service. The letters give an intimate insight into Heg's deep love for his family and his personal qualities as an engaged, strong, and vigorous regimental leader. He affectionately lets Hilda know, "I am glad to hear that you are a good girl." In another letter he asks Hilda: "How is the Piano? Has your little fingers learned to play it yet? When I come back next time I expect you to play *Old John Brown* for me." Edmund gets the following encouragement: "You must learn to ride horseback on the mare—and I will let you keep her for your pony." There is also practical advice, as in regard to the general store the family owned in Waterford. On April 24, 1863, Heg writes to "Dear Edmund," asking: "Are you going to the German School yet? I want you to learn the German language— and not to forget the Norwegian—you will see that it is necessary if we shall keep store."

In a letter to Gunild the summer of 1863, the final paragraph reads: "Tell Dear Hilda that I like her new Dress first rate. But I have no time to write to her. I hope you will not neglect to let her take music lessons. I have more anxiety about Edmund & Hilda receive a good education than anything else."[2]

Island Number Ten

The Fifteenth Wisconsin engaged in several major battles. The first major military action was the siege of Island Number Ten along with

J. Edmund and
Hilda Heg in 1862.
Courtesy Lori
Coffey

Gunild Heg. Courtesy
James T. Heg

Dear Edmund   July 7th 1863

I get any few letters from you.
Why dont you write to me oftener? I wish you would
tell me what sort of a celebration you had on the
4th and how the wheat up on the farm looks—
Do you want me to build a Store on Mas Lot?
One that you could keep store in— in company
with me—? If you will learn to write well, and
be a smart man— I shall have to do as Heage has
done— take you in Partnership with me— and start
a good big store. In your next letter you
may send me a few Postage Stamps— And I want
you to send Mothers Photograph with Cam if you
can get her to take it— I do not care about a
Degaurretype— I want a good Photograph—
want you to see that she puts on her best cloths
and dresses up like a Generals wife— I would
like to get Nebbys Picture too— and if the little
rascal wont send me his picture I shall have
to give him a good spanking when I come home
Nebby must write to me too.
            Good Bye my Boys—
                    From your Pa'lla—

Dear Hilda.   I have time to write a letter to
you to day— but I will write to you to morrow or
next day. I am glad to hear you have a music Teacher.
I know you will be a nice young by the time

Letter from Hans Heg to his children, Edmund and Hilda. Norwegian-
American Historical Association

the Twenty-Seventh Illinois Infantry Regiment on March 15, 1862. Located near New Madrid at the southern Missouri boundary, the island was so named because it was the tenth Mississippi River island south of the Ohio River. Colonel Heg wrote some of his early letters aboard the steamboat *Graham* on the Mississippi, others from Camp Solberg, where the Fifteenth was stationed. In his letter to Gunild dated March 20, Heg showed great self-confidence and a tendency to boast about military achievements: "There is no Wisconsin Regiment that has got along any faster than the 15th, We came right out of camp—took command at Birds Point—from there was ordered right into one of the most important expeditions started since the war commenced."

It should also be noted that on March 31, a portion of the regiment partook in an attack on a rebel camp near Union City, to the east of Hickman, Kentucky. Sailing up the Mississippi from New Madrid, the Fifteenth landed at Hickman and marched to Union City. Close to the city, the Fifteenth surprised a band of rebels; Heg's forces routed the rebels and destroyed their camp and its contents, capturing about a hundred horses and mules and several wagons. Company G captured a battle flag from the "secesh," a nickname and sometime insult for Confederate soldiers. The Confederate battle flag, on which was inscribed, "C.S.H.C., [Hill's Cavalry,] Victory or Death," was sent to Governor Louis P. Harvey (who had succeeded Alexander Randall in January 1862) of Wisconsin as a trophy. They then rejoined the regiment's men stationed at New Madrid.

In his letter dated April 1, Heg reassures Gunild that "I have a strong faith, that I shall get through this unharmed. I have already now gained much credit for what I have done." He reminds her that she has reason to feel proud of her husband. In his letter dated on Island Number Ten, April 9, Heg assures Gunild that the island "is ours, and your humble servant was one of the first to raise the American

Flag over the fortifications." Heg gained valuable experience as acting brigadier general on the island, at one time commanding in addition to his own regiment the Twenty-Second Missouri and the Seventh Wisconsin and Second Illinois.

The Union's gunboats had by then been bombarding the strongly fortified island for three weeks, but there was no indication that the Confederate forces would surrender. The siege was a stalemate. But the Confederates had abandoned New Madrid on March 14. On April 7, 1862, Island Number Ten with its garrison of over five thousand surrendered without bloodshed. The Fifteenth Wisconsin and the Forty-Second Illinois regiments landed on the island. Five hundred men who had not been able to escape across the river became prisoners of war. Fleeing rebels were also captured. Camp Randall in Wisconsin was used as a prisoner-of-war camp. There was in addition a significant booty of large and small cannons and a large storehouse with provisions. Left behind to garrison the island were about 150 men of companies G and I of the Fifteenth and men of company L of the Second Illinois Cavalry.

April 7 was the second day of the far bloodier Battle of Shiloh, and as a consequence the campaign for Island Number Ten lost public notice. But the surrender of Island Number Ten ended the struggle for control of the Upper Mississippi River, and the Union victory signified the ultimate Confederate defeat in the Mississippi Valley.[3]

The Battle of Perryville

A historical narrative focusing mainly on major battles recounts the Fifteenth's successes and failures but overlooks the regiment's collateral activities in the war. Over the course of its widespread geographic engagement was a constant routine of camp and march. Alongside the more significant milestones were a substantial number of severe military engagements and even more skirmishes with the loss of life. The men of the regiment became veterans.

During the summer and autumn of 1862 Heg and his command moved from place to place; two companies were left at Island Number Ten and the regiment was thus reduced in size. The course the regiment took on its march to Perryville can be tracked through Heg's letters to his wife written at camps along the way. On July 20 the regiment was assigned to Colonel William Carlin and the brigade infantry he led in General C. S. Hamilton's division. In Colonel Heg's letter dated August 18, 1862, at a camp near Iuka, Mississippi, he informs Gunild of a long march ahead. And on August 21 the Fifteenth marched with General Jefferson C. Davis's division and reached Nashville, Tennessee, on September 8.

The long march resumed on the eleventh, and on the twenty-sixth the regiment and division entered Louisville, Kentucky. As Heg relates in his letter to Gunild that same day, on the march they had seen the enemy "and been drawn up in line of Battle several times, but every time they have fled." E. B. Quiner in his *Military History of Wisconsin* relates how the men "entered Louisville, tired, hungry, ragged and footsore from their long march." Heg has the following account: "We marched through the city to day, as dusty and ragged as any one could be—but the cheers and hurrahs they gave us showed that we were not thought of any less for being dirty. The girls came out and distributed water, cakes and other articles to the boys along the streets." Heg continues: "My Regiment went through singing Norwegian Songs, and attracted more attention than any other Rgt. that passed." Heg describes in his letter to Gunild the series of forced marches of more than four hundred miles. In spite of the severity of these marches, Heg assures his wife, "I am as fine as a Fiddle—but very tired."

They were by then designated as the Ninth Division of the Army of Ohio, and the brigade as the Thirty-First under Colonel Carlin, consisting of the Twenty-First and Thirty-Eighth Illinois, 101st Ohio, Fifteenth Wisconsin, and Second Minnesota Battery. On October 7 Heg writes to Gunild, "My Dear Wife," to tell her that they were near the enemy, running ahead of them, and they had captured "a good many of their men that fell back." "We must undoubtedly have a big Battle here in Kentucky," Heg writes, concluding, "I don't see how the Rebels can avoid it."

The following day, October 8, the Battle of Perryville was fought in the Chaplin Hills west of Perryville, Kentucky. In a letter dated October 10, Colonel Heg informs Gunild that "Day before yesterday we fought a big Battle." The good news was that even though he had been through it, he was unhurt and, still better, not a single man of the Fifteenth was wounded, even though they had chased the rebels "through showers of Bullets and Cannon Shot." Regardless of Heg's reassuring message, the Battle of Perryville turned out to be the site of one of the bloodiest Civil War battles; it was the largest battle fought in Kentucky. The combat is described in some unsettling detail by William DeLoss Love, including the following disquieting vision: "At length, after hundreds had fallen and were weltering in their blood, or were already stiffened in death, the stillness of darkness came over the sanguinary field of Chaplin Hills, the yet living soldiers slept on their arms, with their dead comrades around them." Simply listing the number of casualties obscures the grim reality of war.

The Confederate troops were under the command of General Braxton Bragg of the Army of Mississippi and the Union forces under Major General Don Carlos Buell of the Union Army of the Ohio. Kentucky had a divided loyalty. Its early declaration of neutrality failed, and the state had troops that fought for the slave states and also troops that supported the Union. Kentucky was one of four loyal border states that stayed with the Union. The other three were Missouri, Maryland, and Delaware. As previously indicated, even though Missouri and Kentucky never seceded, they were admitted to the Confederacy as member states.

As portrayed in *The Civil War and Reconstruction*, the battle of Perryville, October 8, 1862, represented the climax of the Union's early campaign in the West. General Bragg intended to retake the state of Kentucky. His northward march from Chattanooga developed into an ambitious invasion of Kentucky. If successful, Bragg's offensive would have significant political and military implications. In response, Major General Buell entered Louisville, where fresh recruits joined his army. In this first encounter, neither side could claim the battle as victory, but since the invading Confederate Army was forced to withdraw, the advantage was with the North. The Battle of Kentucky, an alternate name for Perryville, was considered a Union victory, especially since Bragg and his troops withdrew to Tennessee shortly after the battle. For the remainder of the war, the Union retained control of the state of Kentucky and the Tennessee River—a strategic waterway.

Colonel Hans Christian Heg and the Fifteenth Wisconsin, along with the other regiments in the Thirty-First Brigade, engaged in military action as ordered and by command. There are several detailed depictions of hostile encounters. Quiner in his military history covers the raging battle the Fifteenth took part in on October 8. In a long letter to Gunild on October 13, Heg reiterates the same confrontational event. Both Quiner and Heg provide a lasting insight into life on the battlefield. Heg relates how the Fifteenth together with the Thirty-First Brigade lined up on top of a hill where they could see "the whole Battle field at a time when it was raging the hardest." "It was a sight I never will forget," Heg wrote to his wife. "While standing and looking on—Col. Carlin rode up and ordered me to advance,"

Heg continued, explaining that the balls were then flying around him and the men of the Fifteenth.

They were ordered by Colonel William Carlin to overpower the enemy. As it turned out, the Fifteenth Wisconsin and the Twenty-First Illinois initially confronted the heavy fire from the enemy's cannon alone. Later the balance of the brigade joined them, and they began capturing some one hundred prisoners and wagons loaded with ammunition. Then the order came to go back about one mile and stay during the night. When they started after the enemy the next morning, the rebels had left. "Notwithstanding their exposure," Quiner concludes, "the Fifteenth escaped without having a man wounded." However, when Heg, together with Dr. Stephen Himoe, visited the battlefield, he discovered an awful sight. He recognized the great loss of life among the men in the brigade. The First, Tenth, Twenty-First, and Twenty-Fourth Wisconsin Regiments had also been in the fight October 8 and were, Heg writes, "mostly all badly cut up." He lets Gunild know the morbid fact that the rebels left all their dead, except officers, and nearly one thousand wounded.[4]

The Battle at Stones River

The campaigns of 1862, in which Colonel Hans Christian Heg and the Fifteenth Wisconsin partook, culminated with the Battle at Stones River—also known as the Battle of Murfreesboro—in Tennessee on December 30, 1862–January 2, 1863. The Confederate troops were led by General Braxton Bragg, as they had been at the Battle of Perryville, and the Union Army by Major General William Starke Rosecrans.

Fighting in the Army of the Cumberland, the Fifteenth Wisconsin experienced its greatest battle up to that time. Eighty-five soldiers of the Fifteenth were killed or wounded and thirty-four missing. Dashing in front of the men in battle, Colonel Heg had his horse shot underneath him and was injured, though not wounded, by the fall. It is important to recognize, as Waldemar Ager writes, that a great many of the men in the Fifteenth had poor knowledge of English and were frightened of hospitals and everything foreign to them. Ager explains: "They felt most at ease among their own kind and were reluctant to be ill. As those on the battlefield frequently 'stood' too long, so they also 'went' sick too long. What happened when they sought help was that it was often too late."

Field officer Lieutenant Colonel David McKee was among the killed, as was Captain John Ingmundson of Company E. Their loss, as P. G. Dietrichson underscores, created much grief, which certainly must also have been the case for the other men lost in battle. McKee was of Irish descent and had been a Democratic member of the Wisconsin legislature, but left his political party because of his strong antislavery principles. Major Ole E. Johnson succeeded McKee as lieutenant colonel.

The men in the Fifteenth, in their camp in Nashville, had engaged in occasional skirmishes until December 26, when they marched in company with the forces of General Rosecrans to take part in the battle at Stones River.

Letters to Gunild, dated January 4 and 6, in which Heg tells of the Battle at Stones River are among the most remarkable and memorable in the collection, according to Blegen. They are lengthy communications, wherein Heg assures Gunild that in spite of it all, he is safe and well.

The Fifteenth Wisconsin Regiment was in William Carlin's brigade. The evening of December 30 the regiment, serving on the federal right, was turned back by a furious Southern attack with heavy loss of lives. "My Dearest Wife," Heg begins on January 4, "We have fought a terrible Battle, and lost a great number of men. My noble Regiment is badly cut up. We were in Three heavy engagements, first on Tuesday evening, when I lost 40 and 50 men killed & wounded. . . . I had my big Horse shot from under me. On the next day we fought twice. . . . I will give you the names of the killed, wounded and missing in Co. C for information to their friends." Heg then lists the names of the missing men from Muskego.

The letters reveal as well Colonel Heg's personal qualities. Blegen, based on the correspondence, describes Heg as a man with a sturdy faith in himself, with a desire for glory for himself and his regiment, and with a tendency to boast. Considering the circumstances Colonel Heg faced, these are all good as well as normal human attributes. In a letter to Gunild on January 4, Heg writes: "I have passed through thus far unhurt and Providence will yet bring me safely through the struggle. I have been in the thickest of the fight and led my men wherever they have fought, The official account of my action will be no disgrace to you or me."

Colonel Heg was without any question recognized for his wartime bravery and leadership. William Carlin, the brigade commander, wrote: "While every field officer under my command did his duty faithfully, Colonels Alexander and Heg, in my opinion, proved themselves the bravest of the brave." Knud Langeland explains further that "In the memorable battle at Stone River, [Heg] conducted himself in a manner that to a high degree captivated the attention of his supervisors." Langeland emphasizes Heg's bravery, stating, "he never encouraged his soldiers to go where he himself was not willing to lead them."

The Union troops, after the first hard day of fighting, spent the night on the battlefield, resting on their arms in the severe cold without fire. On the morning of December 31, the regiment was in line of battle. The fight was renewed and continued on January 2. On that day another Confederate assault was repelled by overwhelming Union artillery fire. General Bragg withdrew the Confederate troops.

In a letter to Gunild dated January 9, Heg observes: "On Friday afternoon, the 2d, they [the rebels] made their last desperate attack, waiting till about an hour and a half before sundown, in order to have the advantage of the night in case of failure. Our lines wavered at first, but it was only temporary, the rebels were forced to give away in disorder." General Major Rosecrans claimed victory, though a rough victory, with a heavy loss of lives. Perhaps not a great success, it nevertheless lifted Union morale.[5]

The Battle of Chickamauga

The Fifteenth Wisconsin Regiment remained in a camp near Murfreesboro and entered into a period of inactivity save for some brief military engagements. In February, while Colonel William Carlin went home for a month, Heg was given command of the Second Brigade. On February 10, Heg writes to Gunild about a two-week military excursion to Franklin, Tennessee, and the rebel forces' long control in that part of the state but, in high spirits, affirms, "the rebel forces are leaving Tennessee and going south." On February 14 he is "once more back in my old tent and at our old camp."

Liberating the enslaved was a constant Union objective. In a letter dated December 21, 1862, published in the *Milwaukee Sentinel* on January 5, 1863, Heg writes: "If the emancipation after the first of January next shall be carried into effect, the negroes will have to be taken care of in some way by the government, at least for a while, by employing them on the confiscated plantations, where at the same time they ought to be educated to take care of themselves, and made to understand their duties as freemen."

President Abraham Lincoln issued the Emancipation Proclamation on January 1, 1863. The proclamation liberated enslaved people in states that had seceded from the Union, leaving slavery untouched in the loyal border states. The promised freedom depended on Union military victory. The proclamation thus did not end slavery in the entire nation, but it was a great inspiration for Americans in the free states, as freedom was expanded with every advance of federal troops. The proclamation accepted Black men into the Union Army and Navy, and the federal government began the process of recruiting and enlisting African Americans into the official ranks of Union soldiers. By the end of the war, some 180,000 Black soldiers had fought for the Union and for freedom. But discrimination still prevailed. The segregated African American regiments were designated as United States Colored Troops, led by white officers. African American troops encountered little opportunity to advance within the ranks. Nevertheless, the proclamation represents a milestone along the road to slavery's final destruction and is one of the great documents of human freedom.

On May 1 Colonel Heg was given permanent command of the Third Brigade of the First Division, Twentieth Army Corps by General Rosecrans. In a letter to Gunild, written that same day, Heg told of his new command of the Third Brigade, which had three regiments, a fourth soon to be added; it had one battery and a company of cavalry. Heg wrote proudly how he fixed up his headquarters in grand style, and that he and the staff officers had splendid tents. The Fifteenth was transferred to the Third Brigade with Lieutenant Colonel Ole C. Johnson in command. The Eighth Kansas Infantry was a regiment in this brigade, and when Colonel Hans Christian Heg was killed at Chickamauga, Colonel John Martin of the Eighth Kansas took command.

Colonel Heg's extensive correspondence back home throughout his military service is truly noteworthy. He finds time and energy to communicate with Gunild and their children regardless of dire wartime circumstances, even after long days of tiresome military duties, occasionally admitting that he is tired and needs to go to bed.

The letters give information about his own activities and about war-time circumstances. Befitting family correspondence, it is personal and private in tone. From his tent in Murfreesboro he proposes Gunild pay him a visit, which suggests he feels it will be safe to do so. In his letter of April 1, Heg writes that he has given up the idea of having Gunild visit him, on the advice of General Rosecrans, and as a gag suggests she wait until he is a general. In his missive dated April 12, Heg enclosed a letter from Søren Bache about a potential trip to Norway, and in a following letter he writes: "The children must learn Norwegian. Tell them that if they do not learn to speak Norwegian they can not go with us." A remarkable optimism charac-terizes Heg's correspondence back home, with promises of joyful family events, even a lengthy transatlantic voyage to the ancestral homeland.

In several letters Hans Heg complained about the tediousness of camp life. He expected to be home by the fall of 1863 and predicted with great anticipation that by then the war would have ended. In the summer of 1863 the nonaction after Murfreesboro came to an end, and General Heg's Third Brigade engaged in the campaign that led to Chickamauga. They left the neighborhood of Murfreesboro on June 24. The army engaged in a long march, but according to Quiner, "nothing occurred of much historical importance, in which the Fif-teenth was engaged." Heg's letters tell of these marches in June and July, as General Rosecrans confronted Bragg and the Confeder-ate Army. On August 29 the brigade reached the Tennessee River near Caperton Ferry, where pontoon boats were put in place, and the Third Brigade was distinguished as the first to cross the river. The Fifteenth Wisconsin was the first regiment to enter the enemy's country, south of the Tennessee River. On August 30 Heg wrote to tell Gunild that his brigade had the honor of crossing the river in advance of the army and to lay pontoons. "My whole Brigade in the

Boats," he continued, "expecting every moment to be shot at, But all went well."

Cozzens relates how Heg led that first crossing of the Tennessee River: "At midnight on the twenty-eighth, his men silently assembled on the riverbank under a bright, cool, moonlit sky. The campfires of Rebel pickets flickered on the opposite bank, five hundred yards distant; none knew how many Confederates lay in wait behind them." In a detailed description of the crossing and the landing, quoting Heg, Cozzens relates how "the gentle swishing of oars and barking of commands broke the morning stillness and the startled" Rebels, "when the boats landed[,] darted up the bluffs, leaving behind burning campfires and half-eaten ears of corn."

Heg's letter has no foreboding of the bloody battles and savage fighting at close quarters just a couple of weeks ahead at Chickamauga. Instead he predicts that Gunild must not expect him home until the Union troops have taken Chattanooga. Ager portrayed Chickamauga thus: "On September 18, 1863, it was merely a tiny unknown river in a remote Georgia valley"; the following day, on September 19, "it was known to the thousands . . . as a sinister word that is now inscribed with blood on the pages of history."

In an appendix of some fourteen pages, Cozzens presents the "Opposing Forces in the Chickamauga Campaign"—a lengthy list with symbolic impact as a Civil War document. Listed first is the Army of the Cumberland, commanded by Major General William S. Rosecrans. Heg became commanding officer of the Third Brigade. Lieutenant Colonel Ole C. Johnson had command of the Fifteenth Wisconsin. Cozzens describes Heg as a gifted young volunteer in the Army of the Cumberland. He praises Heg as an enlightened reformer and for applying a brand of discipline with his first army command as he had done as state prison commissioner. The list of Union and Confederate armies in itself bears witness to the massive military confrontations at each battle during the Civil War, and the heavy loss of life. Cozzens's lists includes officer casualties—killed, mortally wounded, wounded, and captured. The Battle of Chickamauga, fought along the west bank of the Chickamauga River, became one of the bloodiest of the war.

The Fifteenth Wisconsin was one of five infantry regiments from the state of Wisconsin that took part in the great two-day Battle of Chickamauga, fought between the Army of the Cumberland under Major General Rosecrans and the Confederate Army of Tennessee under General Bragg. The Union forces lost a total of 16,971 men in this battle. Rosecrans suffered a terrible defeat at Chickamauga Creek on September 19 and 20. Quiner's detailed description covers several pages. The First Division, led by General Jefferson Davis—where Heg's Third Brigade and the Fifteenth Wisconsin both belonged— was ordered to march, and the military units engaged in a battle that had great loss of life and many wounded survivors. Quiner delineates the sharp fighting, the formation of battle lines, attacks, and counterattacks. The Fifteenth, then at the front, was mistaken for a rebel regiment by reinforcements to the Thirty-Fifth Illinois regiment, who opened fire, while the enemy began a heavy assault on the other side. Placed under "galling fire," as Quiner has it, of both friend and foe, the regiment retired and each man looked out for himself. On the first day of the fighting the Fifteenth Wisconsin lost seven officers and fifty-nine enlisted men.

Colonel Hans Christian Heg, leader of the Third Brigade, became one of the victims. On September 19 at midday, Colonel Heg ordered the Third Brigade into the Battle of Chickamauga, fought on the Viniard Field, property of the Viniard family. Cozzens describes how Heg was playing a risky game, moving his twelve hundred men through a forest thicket without skirmishes and no one to warn them what lay ahead. With federal troops arriving, there were heavy

Colonel Hans Christian Heg at Chickamauga. Herbjørn Gausta, ca. 1915.
Vesterheim Norwegian-American Museum

losses for the Confederates. At this point Cozzens sees the Fifteenth Wisconsin as a regiment in name only, since disease and battle losses had greatly reduced its ranks. Several historical accounts portray Heg in the thick of the fighting. His successor, Colonel John A. Martin, noted in his official report that Colonel Heg had cheered the brigade by his gallantry. He was everywhere present and, as Blegen states, "His coolness and ability to spur men on to hard effort did not desert him in the stress of the battle." At a late hour of the day, Colonel Heg rode forward, swinging his hat to lead his brigade against the enemy. A sharpshooter fired and Heg was pierced by a bullet in the abdomen. Private Lars Larsen rushed forward in the shower of bullets to help him get off his horse and to safety. His fall was near Viniard Field, where a monument in his honor was later raised.

Several officers of the Fifteenth, including Lieutenant Colonel Ole C. Johnson, visited Heg at the federal field hospital close to Chickamauga. Johnson had greetings from the regiment: "the boys of the Fifteenth would have been glad to see you." Colonel Heg was very happy that they had performed their duty to the last. The Fifteenth's surgeon Stephen Himoe attended to him during his time at the hospital. Colonel Heg died shortly before noon on the following day, September 20, 1863. His death was deeply mourned in the regiment and in the brigade.

Emigranten on October 12, 1863, published and edited by C. F. Solberg, who knew Colonel Heg personally and had warmly supported him in organizing the Fifteenth, reacted with surprising serenity to the news of Chickamauga. Solberg announced casualties and prisoners and gave a brief sketch of the regiment, but said nothing about Heg's military career. *Fædrelandet* (The Fatherland), the second Norwegian-language newspaper during the Civil War, launched in La Crosse, Wisconsin, on January 14, 1864, in a belated account, to quote Arlow Andersen, "was more sensitive to the Norwegian military contribution and more openly appreciative of Heg's symbolic role." Both journals' lack of high recognition of Colonel Heg is unusual considering the esteem and praise that was his lot elsewhere. Andersen suggests the editorial views might be conditioned by Northern military failures during the first two years of the war. During the last two years, more positive news from the battlefront gave greater reason for acclaim. Throughout the conflict the press exhibited critical and intelligent loyalty to Lincoln and the Union.

The state of Wisconsin mourned the loss of Colonel Hans Heg. At Chickamauga a pyramid of cannonballs marks the spot where he fell. The greatest sorrow was felt in his home town of Waterford. His body was brought back to Wisconsin, where he was buried with fitting honors by the Masonic fraternity, of which he was a member, in the Old Settlers Cemetery in Waterford. At Colonel Heg's own request his maternal cousin Captain Albert Skofstad of Company D, Fifteenth Wisconsin, accompanied his body home to his grieving family, Gunild, Edmund, Hilda, and Elmer Heg. At the burial, Skofstad writes, "A large group of relatives and friends assembled to pay their last tribute of affection." In "Last Moments of Colonel Heg," published on October 27, 1863, Skofstad attributes positive personal qualities to Heg, concluding with a memorable farewell: "In the homestead burying ground, by the side of his father mother and child, 'he sleeps his last sleep.' Thus has passed from earth a noble man, in the prime of his life, full of buoyant hopes and aspirations. We miss him in our everyday life, in the home circle there is a vacancy that can never be filled."

The Fifteenth Wisconsin lost heavily at Chickamauga—men killed, captured, and wounded. Colonel Ole C. Johnson was one of the men—officers and privates—taken prisoner at the battle on September 20. He was conveyed to the Libby Prison, from which he later

Monument marking the place where Colonel Hans Christian Heg was mortally wounded at the battle of Chickamauga. Wisconsin Historical Society

escaped (more on this story below). On July 24, 1864, Johnson returned to the Fifteenth Wisconsin to be its colonel.

Adding the losses of September 20 to those the day before drops the total number of survivors in the regiment to only 111. The loss might have brought the regiment out of existence. Help was on the way, however. Companies G and I, garrisoned on Island Number Ten, were ordered to rejoin the Wisconsin Fifteenth Regiment. Ben Nelson of Company I relates how the two companies left the island on September 6, taking a steamer up the Mississippi to Cairo. From there they made their way to Chattanooga, forced to take long marches because many bridges had been burned and the railway destroyed. "When we arrived at Chattanooga on September 19," Nelson relates, "a great battle was being fought at Chickamauga, seven miles away."

Monument to the Fifteenth Wisconsin Infantry Regiment at Chickamauga and Chattanooga National Park. Wisconsin Historical Society

He continues: "When we rejoined our regiment on the 21st, there were not many men left—not a hundred. We numbered 156 men, so now there was a total of about 250 left out of almost 1,000."[6]

THE FIFTEENTH AFTER CHICKAMAUGA

The death of Heg on the battlefield at Chickamauga concludes "The Life Story of Colonel Hans Christian Heg," making Heg's biography a historical memorial. In closing, Blegen writes: "So the son of old Muskego passes from the scene—a hero who died for the country." The Fifteenth Wisconsin Regiment persisted as a major legacy of Heg's military service. The regiment's mission did not change, and its history deserves to be conclusively logged. When officially mobilized in 1862, the Fifteenth Wisconsin consisted of 810 privates and about 40 officers—in total 850 men. When it was mustered out December 1864–February 1865, Quiner gives the regiment a strength of 320 men—officers likely included. Loss by death numbered 267; there had also been loss by some missing, a few deserted, and 201 discharged men, the latter mainly as wounded or ill. The regiment gained strength after the Battle of Chickamauga by twenty recruits in 1863 and seventy-six in 1864. The Fifteenth Wisconsin mustered out as a much modified and altered military unit.

After the decisive victory of the Confederate Army under Bragg at Chickamauga—losing 20 percent of its military force in the battle—Rosecrans fell back to Chattanooga, a small city with 2,500 inhabitants. It was the crossroads for four major railroads. The summer of 1863 Rosecrans had outmaneuvered the Confederate Army, forcing General Bragg to relinquish control of the city. The Union Army's retreat from Chickamauga began in the evening of September 21. The Fifteenth Wisconsin joined the Union forces at Chattanooga. The Army of Tennessee under General Bragg laid siege to Chattanooga; two months later federal forces drove the Confederate Army from their positions, giving the North full control of the city. Vital

Confederate supply lines were severed. The Confederate victory at Chickamauga as a consequence became strategically a loss.

John Johnson Thoe of Company K, Clausen's Guards, had regular correspondence with family and friends in Worth County, Iowa, where he was a farmer. He immigrated from Hjartdal in Telemark together with his family at the age of eighteen. He fell at the Battle of New Hope Church in Georgia, in May 1864. In a letter dated in Chattanooga, November 15, 1863, Thoe gives a simple personal report about life as a soldier. He assumes his friend has read all about the Battle of Chickamauga in the newspapers: "Yes, my dear friend, it was a hard battle while it lasted. I have now been in three big battles, but this was one of the hardest. But God be praised and thanked. He held his hand over me, as he always has done, so I got out of it unharmed. . . . We are now at a camp close by Chattanooga and I believe that we are going to stay here for some time. It is quite still here except for some bombs they now and then throw but without doing much harm."

The Battle of Resaca, fought in Gordon and Whitfield Counties, Georgia, from May 13 to 15, 1864, was the first battle of the Union's Atlanta campaign. The Union forces under General William Tecumseh Sherman and the Confederate Army of Tennessee led by General Joseph E. Johnston fought a costly and heavy battle. Beginning May 10, the Fifteenth Wisconsin served on outpost duty as part of an advance military unit. The rebels were then entrenched at a high mountain called Rocky Face. Sherman and other officers considered how the mountain might be taken. By May 13, Ben Nelson writes, the enemy had pulled back and only the outpost guards and the sharpshooters remained. The men left to watch the entrenchments at Rocky Face were ordered to storm the heights. Nelson is proud to report that, led by Sergeant John Wrolstad, the Fifteenth Wisconsin "were the best mountain climbers because we reached the top first."

The persistent battle, ending May 15, might be viewed as inconclusive. Even so, the brave engagement by the much-reduced Fifteenth becomes a significant historical achievement.

The Fifteenth Wisconsin Regiment partook in two more battles before being mustered out: New Hope Church and Kennesaw Mountain. The Battle of New Hope Church, May 25–26, 1864, Georgia, was the second hostile encounter between the Union Army and the Confederate Army during the Atlanta campaign, and under the same leadership as during the Battle of Resaca. For May 25, the first day of the Battle of New Hope Church, Ben Nelson describes "a severe battle [that] raged in which the 15th Wisconsin lost 92 men." He continues, "A great number of our men were taken prisoner while others were killed or wounded."

The Battle of Kennesaw Mountain, about twenty miles northwest of Atlanta, Georgia, was fought June 27, 1864. The Confederate Army failed to halt Sherman's advance on Atlanta. During the Atlanta campaign the Norwegian regiment served in the First Brigade, which comprised nine regiments, commanded by Brigadier General August Willich. Nelson concentrates on the outpost struggles and heavy fighting. The regiment lost several men in the days before the battle on June 27; Nelson lists Daniel Pedersen and Ivar Olson, both of Company I. The Fifteenth Wisconsin Regiment experienced heavy skirmishes later, but no big battles; the men made it to Atlanta on September 29, where the regiment stayed until the next day. Nelson then relates that "we boarded a freight train with 700 prisoners whom we took to Chattanooga." Their time of service expired on December 20.

The fall of Atlanta on September 2, 1864, set the stage for Sherman's March to the Sea and hastened the end of the war. William Tecumseh Sherman, major general of the Union Army, led some sixty thousand soldiers from the captured city of Atlanta on November 15 on a campaign that ended with the capture of the port of Savannah, Georgia, on December 21. Sherman's forces terrorized the country-side, destroying all sources of food and forage, and left behind a hungry and demoralized people. The purpose was to frighten Georgia's civilian population into abandoning the Confederate cause. The March to the Sea was the most destructive campaign against a civilian population during the Civil War.

Events at Appomattox Court House, Virginia, led to Confederate general Robert E. Lee's surrender to Union general Ulysses S. Grant. Federal forces under Grant had cut off the starving and depleted Army of Northern Virginia from any chance at resupply. Further fighting would have been hopeless, and Lee decided to seek terms for surrender from Grant. The terms offered were relatively generous, and Lee signed the surrender at the nearby courthouse. It effectively brought the four-year Civil War to an end. Northern victory preserved the United States as one nation and ended the institution of slavery that had divided the nation from its founding.

Emigranten of April 17, 1865, published the correspondence, translated into Norwegian, between Lee and Grant about surrender—a view into a sensitive situation for both military leaders. Editorially, Solberg reviewed the conflict between the North and South and concluded that "Nothing was more distant from the Union men's thoughts than that the rebels could be victorious." In the issue for April 20, the assassination of Abraham Lincoln on the morning of April 15 was the cataclysmic news. Solberg evidenced great respect for Lincoln and appreciation for his public service. While rejoicing over the recent surrender of General Lee, Solbeg felt pain and bitterness at the death of Lincoln, whom he eulogized as the most beloved president since the days of Washington. Induced by the Union values of the Civil War, the Norwegian American press reflected a growing American patriotism.[7]

PRISONERS OF WAR

In the introduction to *Civil War Prisons*, William Hesseltine reminds the reader of the vast controversy between Northern and Southern partisans over the treatment of prisoners of war. He cautions historians to be objective and separate truth from propaganda in their viewpoints and interpretation of the prisons and the inmates. Hesseltine cites studies that "counted 193,743 Northerners and 214,865 Southerners captured and confined. Over 30,000 Union and nearly 26,000 Confederate prisoners died in captivity . . . over 12 per cent of the captives died in Northern prisons and 15.5 per cent died in the South."

These disturbing statistics, for both the North and the South, do indeed show a great loss of life and should be objectively studied and analyzed. Hesseltine credits the better hospitals in the North than in the South for a lower death rate. The present study will be limited to the Southern strategy and concentrate on the prisoners of Norwegian birth and descent. The story will focus on the Libby Prison in Richmond, Virginia, and Andersonville Prison in Andersonville, Georgia—the two most vile and censurable wartime prisons in the South, most especially Andersonville.

One source for historians to evaluate are the firsthand, antagonistic experience of individual inmates, which deserve to be heard, in spite of some mutual retaliatory, and perhaps overstated, accusations against the enemy. Wartime confinement became a persistent, painful memory throughout these men's lives.

Libby Prison served as the Confederate prison for Union officers; it was located in a three-story brick warehouse on two levels at the waterfront of the James River. The prison had a reputation for being overcrowded and with harsh conditions; lack of sanitation caused diseases and higher mortality rates. Colonel Ole C. Johnson, captured at Chickamauga on September 20, 1863, was conveyed to this Confederate facility. His venture, as related by O. A. Buslett, becomes a detailed account of his capture, time in prison, and escape.

Lieutenant Colonel Johnson gave a postwar speech at Albion College in which he addressed the transfer of enlisted captives to prisons farther south, beginning in December 1863. The battles taking place near Richmond convinced Confederate authorities to seek greater security and food supply for the prisoners elsewhere. "I can forget many things," Johnson began, "but I can never forget how our people looked when they marched past Libby on the way to the train to be sent south." Johnson was one of the prisoners transferred, and four months later he along with fellow prisoners were ordered even farther south. They feared being sent to the notorious Andersonville Prison, which induced Johnson to dare an escape. On May 11, 1864, at Chesterville, South Carolina, he and two Tennessee officers escaped from a railroad boxcar. In his memoirs, Johnson relates how for twenty-nine harrowing days they were on the run behind Confederate lines. On June 11, 1864, the three officers made it to federal troops at Strawberry Plains in eastern Tennessee. Johnson was on leave at home in Wisconsin until returning to the regiment on July 24. He commanded the Fifteenth until it mustered out.

Dread and anxiety of the Andersonville Prison had provoked Johnson's hazardous flight to freedom. *The Civil War and Reconstruction* in the chapter titled "Handling Prisoners of War" analyzes how the South was unable to care for Union captives as the war proceeded, the consequence of a supply systems breakdown and effective officers being needed at the front. The result was horrifying conditions of poor sanitation, malnutrition, and inadequate shelter inside the prisoner-of-war camps. Andersonville was especially notorious. Until the soldiers built huts for themselves, they resided in mosquito-infested tents; "myriad maggots, a contaminated water supply, unbaked rations, inadequate hospital facilities, and lack of sanitation led to high death rates." Union captives who attempted to tunnel their way to freedom were hunted down by bloodhounds.

According to Jerry Rosholt in *Ole Goes to War*, 111 men born in Norway became captives in the infamous Andersonville Prison. Most of them had been captured at the Battle of Chickamauga. Seventy-six of the 111 captives perished in the prison. Forty-nine of those who died were from the Fifteenth Wisconsin Regiment. There were sixty-three soldiers of this regiment in Andersonville; only fourteen survived. Rosholt enumerates the Norwegian soldiers who died as captives in Andersonville and those who survived their time in prison.

Fifteenth Wisconsin captives at Andersonville, when again free, had much to share about their incarceration. Ole Steensland of Company E was in Andersonville more than eleven months and was said to be among the few prisoners who stayed the longest without dying. Revolting memories of Civil War experiences persisted. In August 1900 Steensland delivered a speech in Chicago at a reunion of the Fifteenth Wisconsin Regiment where he dwelt on Andersonville and other Southern prisons. He depicted his own battle engagements and how he was taken prisoner. "Sometimes when I was a prisoner of war," Steensland confessed, "I wished that I had been killed that day so I could have escaped suffering and rotting to death in the southern prisons."

Steensland spoke about the horrors he had witnessed at Andersonville, but in conclusion he chose a more positive tone. "As for the old 'Fifteenth,' I can always say that we always did our duty. I do not know of one prisoner of our regiment who was captured except after a hard fight." Steensland reminded his audience of the men's deep humanity, and asked what they thought "lay closest to our hearts." His own response: "What, in the midst of our misery, engaged most of our conversations? We did not talk about the money we should make once we were free. Oh no! We talked about our mothers, wives, sisters—and sometimes about how well we should eat when we returned home."[8]

THE LEGACY OF COLONEL HANS CHRISTIAN HEG

Colonel Hans Christian Heg died as an American hero and left a lasting legacy which time has only enhanced. His valor and accomplishments are celebrated; indeed, the present biography records his heroic wartime leadership and sacrifice. A second legacy of Heg as a warm and caring person in his human relations and in his response to life's miscellaneous challenges is revealed in his devoted and frequent letters to Gunild and their children. His letters from the Civil War, as Blegen describes them, tell their own story; they portray the man and the soldier and record the history of the Fifteenth Wisconsin Regiment. The letters "constitute the last chapter of a human story."

The Fifteenth Wisconsin and its Civil War campaign encouraged authorship; four of the accounts, written in Norwegian, are cited in the biography. Some commentators have defined these publications as filiopietistic, but even as they show reverence for forebears and tradition, they are not immoderate, and as more or less contemporary accounts they give significant insight and data. They certainly provide evidence of historic enthusiasm in the Norwegian American community for Colonel Hans C. Heg and his Civil War valor.

Reunions became popular events to commemorate how Norwegians contributed to Union victory. Veterans of the Fifteenth met shortly after the Civil War to relive their shared experiences and find comfort in bonding, to celebrate their heroic deeds, and to commemorate the loss of comrades. There were speeches and other edifying presentations, as noted in the 1900 reunion when Ole Steensland shared his memories from the war and imprisonment. The last major reunion of veterans occurred on May 17, 1914, at the Minnesota state fairgrounds, as noted in the first chapter.

Civil War Days to honor Colonel Hans Christian Heg were regularly held at Muskego's Heg Memorial Park, named in his honor. In September 1988 the *Journal Times* had the heading "400 Turn Out to Honor Heg in Norway." In June 1940 the Racine County Colonel Heg memorial committee arranged a "Day in Tribute to [the] Memory [of] Col. Heg."

Following the Civil War, monuments, small and large, were raised to honor war heroes and to memorialize acclaimed battles. At the "15th Wisconsin Memorial Service Chickamauga National Military Park September 17, 1999," a major observance to honor the Fifteenth Wisconsin Regiment and Colonel Heg, wreathes were laid at monuments to both. Special recognition was accorded "the 15th descendants who were able to attend the memorial service." Norwegian author and veteran broadcaster Erik Bye gave an address titled "The Mountains Remember," in which he focused on the Civil War as "a tragic and gruesome conflict."

Colonel Hans Christian Heg had been greatly honored by an impressive pageant at the Norse-American Centennial, celebrated in June 1925 on the fairgrounds between Minneapolis and St. Paul. The Norwegian Society of America (Det norske Selskab af Amerika), formed in Minneapolis in January 1903, was an ambitious effort with a goal of uniting all Norwegians in a national organization to advance Norwegian culture. Waldemar Ager was a major force in the society. But its emphasis on the more refined national expressions prevented it from gaining broad popular support, and consequently it remained an organization for academics and other intellectuals. As a significant undertaking, the society engaged in a nationwide fundraising campaign, which gained momentum in February 1920, to put up a memorial to Colonel Heg.

Noted Norwegian American sculptor Paul Fjelde created a bronze statue of Hans Christian Heg. The statue installed at the Wisconsin State Capitol building in Madison is one of the three casts made at the foundry of Ernst Poleszynski in Oslo, Norway. The statue depicts Colonel Heg standing in his Union Army uniform. Fjelde in describing his work said, "The figure I have created shows a younger Colonel

Heg than his photographs." Fjelde tried "to regain the spirit of youth which must have been his before the cares of war had aged him beyond his years."

The first unveiling of the Heg statue was held at Heg's birthplace, Haugestad in Lierbyen, on June 25, 1925. The local *Middagsavisen* (The Midday Newspaper) reported that ten thousand people had gathered around the monument to attend the festivities by the time the train from Oslo arrived at the Lier railroad station. It carried prominent Norwegian politicians, among them president of the Storting (parliament) Ivar Lykke, representative C. J. Hambro, and other Norwegian and foreign dignitaries. American minister (ambassador) to Norway Laurits S. Swenson also stepped off the train. He was born

Statue of Hans Christian Heg in Lier. The text in Norwegian states: "Norwegian Americans have presented this statue to Lier municipality." Photo by Knut Anders Andersen

Aftenposten, June 25, 1925, reported on the unveiling of the monument in Lier, describing "A festive and moving ceremony" and stating, "The sculptor is hailed." Courtesy Knut Anders Andersen

to Norwegian immigrant parents in New Sweden, Minnesota. They all formed a parade and marched to the statue, where Minister Swenson would conduct the unveiling.

Swenson's speech was much appreciated: "He portrayed the leader and person, the man whose combined qualities made him the obvious leader for others." Swenson expressed the honor he felt by presenting the statue to Lier. Then the "cover fell and the colonel stood there."

"The unveiling became a festive day that will long be remembered by guests as well [as] by hosts," the press claimed. Norwegian Americans in large numbers attended, together with a multitude of local residents. Societies and organizations were well represented, and there were many speeches. Members of the Norwegian Society of

America as well as sculptor Paul Fjelde, both in attendance, were recognized with gratitude. Colonel Heg's double nationality was noted. Bertel Bellesen, president of the large Stavanger Amts Laget, "dwelt on the pride and allegiance Norwegian Americans have to their American citizenship based on the same allegiance they have toward their old homeland, which they will never forget." On this festive day, several speakers highlighted that Colonel Heg, who now was back home again, exemplified this dual loyalty. Commemorating the same hero became a uniting force—even across the Atlantic.

A replica of the statue was erected in 1928 in Heg Memorial Park in Muskego. The Racine County Heg Memorial Committee was organized, encouraged by Norwegian immigrant Nels Bergan, who desired to retain Heg's memory for coming generations. The memorial committee contracted with Paul Fjelde, who created an exact replica of his bronze statue that then stood by the capitol building in Madison. In support of a worthy cause, Fjelde supplied the Muskego replica for just above the actual cost. The nine-foot replica was cast in Oslo and shipped to Muskego.

Land and funds were secured. Lewis Rolfson, a ninety-year-old veteran of Company C, Fifteenth Wisconsin Regiment, recruited by Colonel Heg himself, received the honor of turning the first spadeful of soil in preparation for placing the monument. Rolfson was considered to be the only surviving veteran of the Fifteenth. The statue was erected at the entrance of Heg Memorial Park, and the monument was unveiled on July 4, 1928. Mayor William H. Armstrong of the town of Norway gave the presentation speech. Lewis Rolfson parted the veil covering the statue.

The cast raised in Madison was shipped from Norway in 1925 on the Norwegian America Line (Den norske Amerikalinje) and arrived in New York on August 21, making it to Madison September 3. A delay between arrival and dedication lasted more than a year as a committee worked to raise sufficient funds to purchase and erect a base for the statue.

Two thousand spectators, including Colonel Heg's daughter, Hilda, and Paul Fjelde, attended the statue's unveiling on October 17, 1926, at the Wisconsin State Capitol. Listed as a part of the "Order of Exercises" is the following: "Preceding the singing of America, the sculptor, Mr. Paul Fjelde, of New York, and the officers of the Norwegian Society of America will be presented to the assemblage." Waldemar Ager is given credit for the memorial becoming a reality.

The unveiling address was by Professor Julius E. Olson, the second holder of a professorship in the Scandinavian department at the University of Wisconsin, established in 1869 as the first in America. Standing at the statue in Capitol Park, Professor Olson gave a lengthy eulogy of Colonel Hans Christian Heg, who "ended his career as a martyr of liberty in the great struggle for the preservation of this American Union."

Olson made a point of the fact that it was just one hundred and one years since Norwegian immigrants of modern times began coming to this country. He expanded to include "the immigrant from every nation," stressing that "America's strength and power and influence are due to the result that has been brought about through the intermingling of the blood of many nations." And "How emphatically, how heroically, does this bronze figure of Hans Christian Heg symbolize the immigrant in America" became Olson's inclusive message that by honoring Colonel Heg, "we do honor to ourselves—a cosmopolitan, liberty-loving people, who have transplanted in America the seed from which developed a model commonwealth."

The *Wisconsin State Journal* on October 18, 1926, ran the headline "Heg Statue Unveiling Bares American Ideals" of loyalty and sacrifice as manifested by the place of honor accorded the statue at the "gateway" to the capitol.

The restored memorial statue of Colonel Hans Christian Heg was rededicated on May 29, 2022, at a ceremony near the capitol in Madison, Wisconsin. Photo by Ronald Lovoll

The statue that was vandalized, decapitated, and thrown into Lake Monona on June 23, 2020 (see page 1), was restored and on May 29, 2022, rededicated near the Wisconsin State Capitol in a memorable ceremony. Both the Norwegian and the American flags were hoisted, recognizing Hans Christian Heg's place of birth and the ethnic composition of the Fifteenth Wisconsin Volunteer Infantry Regiment. Heg, honored as "hero, immigrant, civic leader, abolitionist, patriot, husband and father . . . was also the highest-ranking Wisconsin soldier to give his life in the Civil War."[9]

Acknowledgments

I would like to recognize and express my gratitude to a number of people who generously gave their advice and time and in many ways assisted me in my investigation. The pandemic—which limited access to archives and libraries during my two years of research and writing—made me more dependent on generous assistance. I am most grateful for the friendly response to my many inquiries.

As stated in the preface, I appreciated the encouragement by James T. Heg to write the biography of his famed ancestor Colonel Hans Christian Heg and the source material he provided. I also received historical data about Colonel Heg from James P. Heg and Lori Coffey, who in addition provided illustrations. When I served as the Norwegian-American Historical Association's editor, I invited long-time friend Harry T. Cleven to write the introduction to *Colonel Heg and His Boys*. Cleven generously donated important documents to my project. I feel greatly indebted to NAHA board members and staff, most especially to archivist Kristina R. Warner for her untiring and enthusiastic research and for assembling the illustrations and captions, and to executive director Amy L. Boxrud for her encouragement and guidance. I thank earlier and current board members for their support: Debbie L. Miller, former Minnesota Historical Society staff member; Daron William Olson, Indiana University East; and Dennis Gimmestad, chair of the endowment campaign. I also wish to thank editor Anna M. Peterson, Luther College, and Michael Lansing, professor at Augsburg University, for their steadfast support of the project. Mary E. Barbosa-Jerez at the Rolvaag Memorial Library at St. Olaf and her student Sophie Vlahoulis made copies from *Emigranten*, and student Sophia Hayes scanned pages from Karl Jakob Skarstein's history of Norwegians in the Civil War.

In Decorah, Iowa, I spent time at Luther College doing research on Norwegian American newspapers. I do not quite know how to adequately express my gratitude to special collection coordinator Andrea L. Beckendorf and to Luther College librarian Germano G. Streese for their warm welcome and generous assistance. I also wish to thank Hayley Jackson in the Luther College Archives for research assistance. Archivist Jennifer Kovarik at Vesterheim Norwegian-American Museum was most helpful, and later located and transferred relevant images from the Vesterheim collection. As always museum director Chris Johnson and staff gave me a warm welcome.

The generous service and involvement of societies, museums, and libraries in Wisconsin enabled me to produce a publishable manuscript in spite of pandemic restrictions on fieldwork. At the Wisconsin Historical Society, reference librarian Gayle Martinson invested much time in locating research material, as did reference archivist Lee Grady. Business manager Lisa R. Marine was most gracious and helpful in providing relevant images. I also thank reference assistant Jennifer Barth.

Resource Center clerk Rory Graves at the Civil War Museum deserves my gratitude as well, as does librarian Rebecca Leannah at the Racine Public Library. Executive Director Keighton Klos was my helpful contact at the Milton Historical Society and Milton House Museum. I thank Amelia H. Chase, digital assets archivist, Alabama

Department of Archives and History, for her friendly response and
for the images she provided on slavery and the slave trade in Alabama.

My son, Ronald Lovoll, provided transportation that enabled me to
do fieldwork in Wisconsin. Our visits at the Racine Heritage Museum
and at Heg Memorial Park were most productive and pleasant. Mary
Kay Nelson, archivist at Racine Heritage Museum, together with
museum assistants Red Paulin and Darlene A. Young spent several
hours assisting me during my visit to the museum. Executive Director Christopher Paulson gave us a warm welcome and shared insightful information about the museum and Heg Memorial Park.
Paulson's enthusiasm and support, including photos he took throughout the research and writing phase, created a pleasant and productive scholarly investigation. He introduced us to Marilyn Canfield,
who was our knowledgeable guide to the park and later, together
with Anneliese Oswald, made available photos and artistic portray-
als owned by the memorial park for my consideration. Illustrations
were generously provided by individuals and archives during my
research. Only a selection has been reproduced here. I appreciate
the support Lise Løken and Dina H. Tolfsby gave. I am thankful to
Ellen Vollebæk for her enthusiastic engagement in the project.

During a visit to Norway, James T. Heg introduced me to Knut A.
Andersen and Bjørg Andersen. They were among my earliest con-
tacts and were my hosts when I visited Lier. In their correspondence
with me, they shared important historical data about this region
of the country as well as photos. Professor Emeritus Øystein Rian
shared important historical facts about Hans Nielsen Hauge, and
Øyvind Tveitereid Gulliksen responded generously to my queries in
regard to Bø in Telemark and other mountainous districts close by.
Longtime friend Kjetil Flatin and Hans Brattestå forwarded photos
and artistic depictions from Lier and Telemark, again for my consideration. I thank them all most sincerely, and I warmly thank John

Wroughton for the photo he took of Gaustatoppen, and Terje Mikael Hasle Joranger for good advice and a photo showing conditions on board sailing ships.

As with all my publications, my family has been at my side. Son Ronald and daughter-in-law Margit Lovoll and daughter Audrey and son-in-law Helge Syversen have most warmly encouraged and assisted me and expressed their pride in my scholarly enterprise. Margit and Ronald accompanied me to the historic rededication of the Heg statue in Madison on May 29, 2022, for which I am most grateful.

The statement by Minnesota Historical Society Press director Josh Leventhal that it would be an honor to publish the Heg biography gave added motivation. Shannon Pennefeather served as the responsible editor, as she has done in a number of my earlier scholarly works. Her expertise and friendship were much appreciated. I also wish to thank manuscript reviewer Kristin Risley for Civil War expertise and scholarly advice. It is much appreciated.

Notes

Notes to Chapter 1

1. Odd Sverre Lovoll, *A Folk Epic: The Bygdelag in America* (Boston: Published for the Norwegian-American Historical Association by Twayne Publishers, 1975), 119–20; Waldemar Ager, *Colonel Heg and His Boys: A Norwegian Regiment in the American Civil War*, trans. Della Kittleson and Clarence A. Clausen (Northfield, MN: Norwegian-American Historical Association, 2000), 207–9, quote 209.

2. Odd S. Lovoll, *The Promise of America: A History of the Norwegian-American People*, rev. ed. (Minneapolis: University of Minnesota Press, 1999), 300–303, 330; Lovoll, *A Folk Epic*, 166–69, quote 169. See Carl H. Chrislock, "The First Two Centennials, 1914 and 1925," in *Norwegian American Centennial, 1825–1975* (Minneapolis: Norwegian American Sesquicentennial Association, 1975), 34–36, quote 34; Odd S. Lovoll, "The Changing Role of May 17 as a Norwegian-American 'Key Symbol,'" in *Nasjonaldagsfeiring i fleirkulturelle demokrati*, ed. Brit Marie Hovland and Olaf Aagedal (Copenhagen, Denmark: Nordisk Ministeråd, 2001), 65–78. Newspaper clippings in scrapbooks in the Colonel Hans Christian Heg collection, Norwegian-American Historical Association, Northfield, MN (hereafter, NAHA).

Carl Nelson, described as a hardy individual, following the return from the centennial celebration suffered a stroke and died on August 30, 1925. Nelson was born in Oslo, Norway, on July 25, 1829, and immigrated to America together with his wife in 1851. The voyage across the Atlantic took fourteen weeks and four days.

The designation *amt* for a province was in 1918 altered to *fylke*. Many of the administrative units were given new names.

3. Geir Thorsnæs, "Lier," in *Store norske leksikon* på snl.no. Hentet 11, November 2020, fra https://snl.no/Lier; Per Otto Borgen, *Lier Bygdeleksikon* (Drammen, Norway: Forlaget for by- og bygdehistorie, 1997), 121; Rolf Fladby, *Liers historie*, https://www.lier.kommune.no/liers-historie/innhold.htm.

Buskerud *fylke* merged on January 1, 2020, with Akershus and Østfold to form the province (*fylke*) Viken. Vestfold og Telemark merged as a single province on the same date.

Speciedaler was the monetary system in Norway 1816 to 1874, when it was replaced with krone. A speciedaler equaled four kroner.

4. Borgen, *Lier bygdeleksikon*, 76–77, 121, 131, 153; Fladby, *Liers historie*. For the cotter system, see Arnfinn Engen, "Husmannsvesenet på Austlandet," in *Husmannsfolk. Husmannsminne frå Gudbrandsdalen* (Oslo: Tiden forlag, 1979).

Christiania was the name of Oslo from 1624 to 1924 in honor of King Christian IV of Denmark and Norway. In 1925 the Norwegian capital was renamed Oslo.

5. Søren N. Roer, *Slekten fra Nedre Opstad i Rygge gjennom 300 år* (Moss, Norway: Utgitt ved medlemmer av slekten, 1971), 11, 178, 215; Fladby, *Liers historie*; Borgen, *Lier bygdeleksikon*, 76; Theodore C. Blegen, ed., *The Civil War Letters of Colonel Hans Christian Heg* (Northfield, MN: Norwegian-American Historical Association, 1936), 3, quotes 2; Clarence A. Clausen and Andreas Elviken, trans. and ed., *A Chronicle of Old Muskego: The Diary of Søren Bache, 1839–1847* (Northfield, MN: Norwegian-American Historical Association, 1951), ix–xix; Arne Bergsgård, *Norsk historie 1814–1880*, 2nd ed. of Dagfinn Mannsåker and Magnus Skodvin, *Frå 17. mai til 9. april* (Oslo: Det norske Samlaget, 1964), 153–55; Odd S. Lovoll, *Norwegians on the Prairie: Ethnicity and the Development of the Country Town* (St. Paul: Minnesota Historical Society Press, 2006), 104–9, quote 104; copy of the original Norwegian Constitution of 1814; Bjørg and Knut Anders Andersen, letter dated December 10, 2020. Studies cited are Steinar Thorvaldsen, *A Prophet Behind the Plough: Hans Nielsen Hauge and His Ministry* (Tromsø, Norway: University of Tromsø, 2010), and Andreas Aarflot, *Hans Nielsen Hauge, His Life and Message* (Minneapolis: Augsburg Publishing House, 1979).

Rygge, then a municipality, merged with the city of Moss on January 1, 2020.

6. Andres A. Svalestuen, "Emigration from the Community of Tinn, 1837–1907: Demographic, Economic, and Social Background," trans. C. A. Clausen, in *Norwegian-American Studies* 29 (1983): 44–49, quote 48; see H. H. Einung, *Tinn Soga*, vol. 11 (Kragerø, Norway: Eigi Forlag, 1978).

Gaustatoppen is the highest mountain in the province of Vestfold og Telemark in Norway. From the summit there is a broad view of Norway's mainland.

7. Einung, *Tinn Soga*, 499–503; *Telesoga*, November 2011, 22–35; Øyvind Tveitereid Gulliksen, letter dated October 27, 2020; Svalestuen, "Emigration from the Community of Tinn," 85.

8. Theodore C. Blegen, *Norwegian Migration to America, 1825–1860* (Northfield, MN: Norwegian-American Historical Association, 1931), 48–56, 88–89, 93–95, 118–19, quote 81; Blegen, *Civil War Letters of Colonel Heg*, 2–5; Lovoll, *The Promise of America*, 10–13, 14, 16–17, 18, 22–23; Theodore C. Blegen, trans. and ed., *Ole Rynning's True Account of America* (Minneapolis, MN: Norwegian-American Historical Association, 1926), 70–74.

9. Blegen, trans. and ed., *Ole Rynning's True Account of America*, 5–6; Svalestuen, "Emigration from the Community of Tinn," 49, 50–53; Lovoll, *The Promise of America*, 13, 46–47, 51–53; Blegen, *Norwegian Migration to America*, 88–90, 115–21; Odd S. Lovoll, *Across the Deep Blue Sea: The Saga of Early Norwegian Immigrants* (St. Paul: Minnesota Historical Society Press, 2015), 28–29.

10. Blegen, *Civil War Letters of Colonel Heg*, 2–5; Blegen, *Norwegian Migration to America*, 53, 126–28; Clausen and Elviken, trans. and ed., *A Chronicle of Old Muskego*, xii–xiv; Joseph Schafer, "Hans Christian Heg," in *The Wisconsin Blue Book: 1933* (Madison, WI: Democrat Printing Co., 1933), 37–38.

11. Svalestuen, "Emigration from the Community of Tinn," 43, 85; *Telesoga*, 2011, 23–24, 32, quote 23; Einung, *Tinn Soga*, 502, quote 502; Blegen, *Civil War Letters of Colonel Heg*, 249–50; C. A. Clausen, "An Immigrant Shipload of 1840," *Norwegian-American Studies and Records* 14 (1944): 54–65. Gerhard B. Naeseth, "The 1842 Immigrants from Norway," *Norwegian-American Studies* 25 (1972): 225–57, presents a comprehensive record of Norwegian immigrants that year.

12. Lovoll, *The Promise of America*, 14–16, 20–22, 31, 47–51, quote 16; Carlton C. Qualey, *Norwegian Settlement in the United States* (Northfield,

MN: Norwegian-American Historical Association, 1938), 38; Lovoll, *Across the Deep Blue Sea*, 24–33; Odd S. Lovoll, *A Century of Urban Life: The Norwegians in Chicago before 1930* (Northfield, MN: Norwegian-American Historical Association, 1988), 7–8, 12, 42–43; Odd S. Lovoll, "The Great Exodus," in *They Came from Norway: A Sesquicentennial Review*, ed. Erik J. Friis (New York: Norwegian Immigration Sesquicentennial Commission, Inc., 1975), 10–15.

Strip farming in western and southern Norway relates to land distribution in agriculture. In collective farmsteads where every farmer owned or rented a part of the farm, the home fields were divided into small strips and each family maintained rights to both the fertile and marginal fields.

13. Qualey, *Norwegian Settlement in the United States*, 25, 28–29, 32–33, 40–41, 78, 97, 99, 111–12, 129, quotes 14, 39, 44, 97; Blegen, *Norwegian Migration to America*, 85, 88–94, quote 376–77; Lovoll, *The Promise of America*, 51–53, 57, 75, 107, 115, 116–17, 118–22; Theodore C. Blegen, trans. and ed., *Peter Testman's Account of His Experiences in North America* (Northfield, MN: Norwegian-American Historical Association, 1927), 1–4, quote 55; *Emigranten*, July 1, 1853; Lovoll, *Norwegians on the Prairie*, 32–34, 102; Carlton C. Qualey, "A Typical Norwegian Settlement: Spring Grove, Minnesota," *Norwegian-American Studies and Records* 9 (1936): 54–55, quote 55; Odd S. Lovoll, *Norwegian Newspapers in America: Connecting Norway and the New Land* (St. Paul: Minnesota Historical Society Press, 2010), 47, 49.

Notes to Chapter 2

1. Clausen and Elviken, trans. and ed., *A Chronicle of Old Muskego*, xii–xiii, 40–41, quote 41–42; Lovoll, *The Promise of America*, 55–58; Blegen, *Civil War Letters of Colonel Heg*, 4–5; Hjalmar Rued Holand, "Muskego," in *Symra*, Decorah, IA, 1907, 188–89, quotes 188–89; J. Magnus Rohne, *Norwegian American Lutheranism up to 1872* (New York: Macmillan Company, 1926), 46–47; Qualey, *Norwegian Settlement in the United States*, 48–49; *Telesoga*, 2011, 23, 24–25, 26, 30, 32, quotes 24, 25; C. A. Clausen, tr. and ed., *A Chronicler of Immigrant Life: Svein Nilsson's Articles in* Billed-Magazin, *1868–1870* (Northfield, MN: Norwegian-American Historical Association, 1982), 19, quote 19; Ingrid Semmingsen, *Veien mot vest. Utvandringen fra Norge til Amerika 1825–1865* (Oslo: Forlagt av H. Aschehoug & Co. [W. Nygaard], 1941), 288–89.

2. Lovoll, *The Promise of America*, 17–18, 51–55, 55–58; Qualey, *Norwegian Settlement in the United States*, 44–55; Clausen and Elviken, trans. and ed.,

A Chronicle of Old Muskego, 42–43, 99–100, quotes 99, 100; Johan R. Reiersen, "Norwegians in the West in 1844: A Contemporary Account," trans. and ed. Theodore C. Blegen, *Studies and Records* 1 (1926): 118–25, quotes 115, 116; Johan Reinert Reiersen, *Pathfinder for Norwegian Emigrants*, trans. Frank G. Nelson (Northfield, MN: Norwegian-American Historical Association, 1981), quote 187–98; Blegen, *Civil War Letters of Colonel Heg*, 5, 8–9, quote 9; Ella Stratten Colbo, "The Life Story of Colonel Hans Christian Heg," Historic Heg Memorial Park, Racine, WI, 1975, quote 21; Bjørg and Knut Anders Andersen, letter dated December 10, 2020; Knut Gjerset and Ludvig Hektoen, "Health Conditions and the Practice of Medicine among the Early Norwegian Settlers, 1825–1865," *Studies and Records* 1 (1926): 7–8, 17; Blegen, *Norwegian Migration to America*, 128–30, 141, 144–45; Holand, "Muskego," 191; Lovoll, *Norwegian Newspapers in America*, 7–9, 370; Clausen, trans. and ed., *A Chronicler of Immigrant Life*, 87, 108, 113–16, quotes 17, 108, 113; *Wisconsin Blue Book: 1933*, 38, quote 38.

In the introduction to the Civil War letters of Colonel Heg, it is a bit surprising that Blegen refers to Heg's mother only twice, and then without her name, Siri (Sigrid) Olsdatter Heg. In the index she is simply listed as Mrs. Even Hansen.

3. Clausen, trans. and ed., *A Chronicler of Immigrant Life*, 20–21, 88–90, 92, quotes 20, 89; Blegen, *Norwegian Migration to America*, 131; Blegen, *Civil War Letters of Colonel Heg*, 7, quote 7; Lovoll, *The Promise of America*, 81–82, quote 81; Lovoll, *Norwegian Newspapers in America*, 22–24; Carlton C. Qualey, trans. and ed., "Claus L. Clausen, Pioneer Pastor and Settlement Promoter," *Norwegian-American Studies and Records* 6 (1931): 12–13; *Nordlyset*, March 15, 1849; Clausen and Elviken, trans. and ed., *A Chronicle of Old Muskego*, 100–101, 104–5, 120–21, 147–53, quotes 120, 150, 151; Semmingsen, *Veien mot vest*, 334; O. A. Buslett, *Det Femtende Regiment Wisconsin Frivillige* (Trykt hos B. Anundsen, Decorah, IA: Paa Forfatterens Forlag, 1895), 196–99.

The Muskego church was the first Norwegian Lutheran church built in America, but the two churches built by congregations organized by Pastor J. W. C. Dietrichson in Koshkonong were dedicated earlier: the East Church in the town of Christiana on January 31, 1845, and the West Church in Pleasant Spring on December 19, 1844. The Muskego church was in use by the congregation until 1869 and is preserved and located in the park by Luther Seminary in St. Paul, Minnesota.

4. Clausen and Elviken, trans. and ed., *A Chronicle of Old Muskego*, xiii, 159–62, quotes xiii, 161; Semmingsen, *Veien mot vest*, 334–35; Ingrid

Semmingsen, *Norway to America: A History of the Migration*, trans. Einar Haugen (Minneapolis: University of Minnesota Press, 1978), 80–82; Einar Haugen, "Pastor Dietrichson of Old Koshkonong," *Wisconsin Magazine of History* (March 1946): 301–3, 304, quote 304; Blegen, *Norwegian Migration to America*, 131, 162, 248–49, quote 249; Knud Langeland, *Nordmændene i Amerika. Nogle Optegnelser om de Norskes Udvandring til Amerika* (John Anderson & Co., 1880), 74; Lovoll, *The Promise of America*, 53, 72, 75–76, 78–80, 82–87, quote 72; Lovoll, *Norwegian Newspapers in America*, 22–26; J. W. C. Dietrichson, *Reise blandt de norske Emigranter. "De forenede norda-merikanske Fristater"* (Madison, WI: Rasmus B. Anderson, 1846), 27–31, 34–35, 39, 41–43, quotes 30, 34, 39, 43; Rohne, *Norwegian American Lutheranism up to 1872*, 47–51, 64, 66, 69, 70–71, 72–74, 75, 93–94, 112–19, 129–31, 134–35, quotes 16, 43, 66; E. Clifford Nelson, ed., *A Pioneer Churchman: J. W. C. Dietrichson in Wisconsin, 1844–1850* (New York: Twayne Publishers, Inc. for Norwegian-American Historical Association, 1973), 22–23, 146, 149, 179–80, quotes 149, 153, 179–80.

5. Lovoll, *Norwegian Newspapers in America*, 10, 12–14, 17, 19, 35, 349–50; Langeland, *Nordmændene i Amerika*, 94–97; *Nordlyset*, July 29, 1847, February 3, 24, November 16, 1848, June 7, 28, 1849; *Democraten*, October 12, November 9, 1850; Clausen and Elviken, trans. and ed., *A Chronicle of Old Muskego*, 217; Blegen, *Civil War Letters of Colonel Heg*, 10–11, quote 10; Blegen, *Norwegian Migration to America*, 132, quote 132; *Stavanger Amtstidene*, July 16, 1861.

A Scandinavian joint organ, *Skandinavia*, published in January 1847 by an organized Scandinavian society in New York with entries in Dano-Norwegian and Swedish, preceded *Nordlyset* by some months. See Lovoll, *Norwegian Newspapers in America*, 1–15.

6. Lovoll, *Norwegian Newspapers in America*, 34–44, quote 39; Lovoll, *The Promise of America*, 104–5; Langeland, *Nordmændene i Amerika*, 109–10; Arlow W. Andersen, "Lincoln and the Union: A Study of the Editorials of *Emigranten* and *Fædrelandet*," *Norwegian-American Studies and Records* 15 (1949): 85–121; *Emigranten*, January 23, 30, February 20, 1852, January 27, July 24, 1854, April 3, 25, July 22, 1857, January 20, 27, 1858, May 21, September 12, October 24, November 21, 1859, December 3, 1860; Albert O. Barton, "The Beginnings of the Norwegian Press in America," *State Historical Society of Wisconsin. Separate No. 174. From the Proceedings of the Society for 1916* (Madison, WI: The Society, 1916), 200–11, quote 201; Blegen, *Civil War Letters of Colonel Heg*, 58; Ronald Paul Larson, *Wisconsin and the Civil War* (Charleston, SC: History Press, 2017), 14–15.

7. Blegen, *Civil War Letters of Colonel Heg*, 11–14, quotes 11, 12; *Nordlyset*, March 26, 29, May 17, October 11, 1849; diary kept on the journey, 1849, in NAHA's Civil War Collection; letter signed H. Chr. Heg from Weaverville, California, dated October 7, 1849, in NAHA Publication Papers, published in *Nordlyset*, February 23, 1850; Knud Langeland, "Oberst H. C. Heg," in J. A. Johnson, *Det Skandinaviske Regiments Historie (15de Wisconsin Regiment)* (La Crosse, WI: Trykt i "Fædrelandet og Emigranten"s Trykkeri, 1869), 104–9; H. W. Brands, *The Age of Gold: The California Gold Rush: The New American Dream* (New York: Anchor Books, 2003), 3, 15–17, 45, 378; Susan Lee Johnson, *Roaring Camp: The Social World of the California Gold Rush* (New York: W. W. Norton & Co., 2000), 68, 69, 70–71, 90–92; *Democraten*, August 31, 1850.

Sutter's mill was owned by John Sutter, a Swiss settler in California. He formed a colony on the Sacramento River, the California governor granting him nearly fifty thousand acres. He hired carpenter James Marshall to help build the sawmill.

8. *Wisconsin Blue Book: 1933*, 38; Colbo, "The Life Story of Hans Christian Heg," 21, 22; Blegen, *Civil War Letters of Colonel Heg*, 16, 50–51n, 249–50; "Charles N. Fowler," https://en.wikipedia.org/wiki/Charles_N._Fowler; Elmer Ellsworth Heg information courtesy James T. Heg.

In 1856 Hans Christian and Gunild Heg adopted six-year-old Even E. Olson, born June 6, 1850, in Lier, Norway. Even came to America in 1853 with his family: father Christian Olson, mother Martha Evensdatter, and siblings Maren Randine (born in 1843), Ole (born in 1845), and Anne (born in 1848). They settled in Racine. By 1855 Even's father had died. His mother likely died giving birth to a daughter after the 1855 census was taken. The children were then split up. As an adoptive son he became Even Heg. When Hans Heg went to war, Even Heg stayed with the Ole Heg family in Waterford. In 1865 he moved to Racine and went to work for the J. I. Case Threshing Machine Company. He married Anna Curry, who was born in Ireland. They had three children. As an adult Even used the name Olson. He died October 1, 1924, and is buried at Mound Cemetery in Racine. Information from Marilyn Canfield and Dee Anna Grimsrud.

Notes to Chapter 3

1. Blegen, *Civil War Letters of Colonel Heg*, 11, 15, quotes 11, 15; J. A. Johnson, *Det Skandinaviske Regiments Historie*, 104–9; *Emigranten*, September 12, 1859; Colbo, "The Life Story of Colonel Hans Christian Heg," 21–22;

"6th Wisconsin Legislature," https://en.wikipedia.org/wiki/6th_Wisconsin _Legislature.

2. *Emigranten*, September 12, 1859; Nicholas C. Burckel, ed., *Racine: Growth and Change in a Wisconsin County* (Racine, WI: Racine County Board of Supervisors, 1977), 48, 50; *The Grassroots History of Racine County* (Racine, WI: Racine County Historical Museum, 1978), n.p.

"Wisconsin. Justice of the Peace (Eau Claire): Justice Dockets, 1873–1919," Library-Archives Division, Wisconsin Historical Society, Madison, WI, provides an online definition of the office of the justice of the peace. It was abolished in Wisconsin in 1966.

3. Elizabeth Gaspar Brown, "Poor Relief in a Wisconsin County, 1846–1866: Administration and Recipients," *American Journal of Legal History* 20 (April 1976): 79, 80; "Racine County Poor Farm," *The History of Racine and Kenosha Counties* (Chicago: Western Historical Co., 1879), 328–30, quote 328; *Journal of the Proceedings of the Board of Supervisors of Racine County, at their Annual Session, Commencing November 13, 1855* (Racine, WI: A. C. Sandford, Advocate Office, 1855), 1, 2, 3, quote 3: Blegen, *Civil War Letters of Colonel Heg*, 15, quotes 15, 16; *Commemorative Biographical Record of Prominent and Representative Men of Racine and Kenosha Wisconsin* (Chicago: J. H. Beers & Co., 1906); 1850 census information provided by Rebecca Leannah, Racine Public Library; Colbo, "The Life Story of Hans Christian Heg," quote 22.

4. Johnson, *Det Skandinaviske Regiments Historie*, 105–6, quote 105; "Wisconsin and the Republican Party: A New Vision for the United States," Wisconsin Historical Society online; Lovoll, *Norwegian Newspapers in America*, 26–31; *Den norske Amerikaner*, September 29, 1855, August 16, November 1, 15, December 27, 1856, March 14, April 4, 18, May 27, 1857; *Emigranten*, August 24, 1855, October 3, November 7, 21, 1856, September 16, 1857, September 5, 12, October 3, 10, 1859, quotes January 8, 16, 1857, September 5, October 10, November 21, 28, 1859; Ernest Bruncken, "Political Activity of Wisconsin Germans, 1854–60," in *Proceedings of the State Historical Society of Wisconsin* (1901), 191–92, 197–98, 199, quote 190; Joseph Schafer, "Know-Nothingism in Wisconsin," *Wisconsin Magazine of History* (September 1924): 8–9, 12, 13, 14–15, 19, 20, quotes 9, 12; *The Wisconsin Blue Book: 1962* (Madison: State of Wisconsin, 1962), 71, 74–75; Blegen, *Civil War Letters of Colonel Heg*, 16–18, quotes 16–17; *Stavanger Amtstidende*, quote July 16, 1861, translated by the author.

5. "Wisconsin State Prison (Waupun Correctional Institution)," Dictionary of Wisconsin History, online; *Stavanger Amtstidende,* quote July 16, 1861; "En Tur til Wisconsins Statsfængsel," in *Emigranten,* August 5, 19, 1861. "Report of the State Prison Commissioner," Waupun, Wisconsin, October 1, 1860, 2–10, quotes 4; "Annual Report of the State Prison Commissioner," September 20, 1861, 1–4; Letter to W. H. Watson, May 7, 1861—all at Wisconsin Historical Society, Madison, WI. Blegen, *Civil War Letters of Colonel Heg,* 18–19, 20–21; Johnson, *Det Skandinaviske Regiments Historie,* 103–6.

6. "Booth, Sherman Miller 1812–1904," Wisconsin Historical Society online; "Sherman Booth," https://en.wikipedia.org/wiki/Sherman_Booth; "In Re: Booth," 1–2, https://www.wicourts.gov/courts/supreme/docs/famous cases01.pdf; "Fugitive Slave Act of 1850," https://en.wikipedia.org/wiki/Fugitive_Slave_Act_of_1850; Ben Manski, "State Power against the Slave Power: How Wisconsin Warred on Slavery and Won," *Liberty Tree Journal* 1, no. 3 (Summer 2006); "A Journey from Slavery to Freedom: A Brief Biography of Joshua Glover," Wisconsin Historical Society online; A. J. Beitzinger, "Federal Law Enforcement and the Booth Case," *Marquette Law Review* (Summer 1957); Richard N. Current, *The Civil War Era, 1848–1873, The History of Wisconsin,* vol. II (Madison: State Historical Society of Wisconsin, 1976), 270–73; *Waupun Times,* August 5, 8, 1860; *Waupun Prison City Newspaper,* August 10, 1860; O. H. La Grange, "The Booth War in Ripon: Personal Reminiscences," and "Brevet Major George," NAHA. Some of the documents in this section were located and extensively researched by Kevin Dier-Zimmel. Recognized with gratitude.

7. Andersen, "Lincoln and the Union," 85, quote 85; Fergus M. Bordewich, *Bound for Canaan: The Epic Story of the Underground Railroad, America's First Civil Rights Movement* (New York: Harper Collins, 2005), 54, 56, 79, 104–8, 135–36, 143–46, 147, 155, 161–62, 196–97, 202, 230, 236, quote 236; "Experience History: The Underground Railroad in Wisconsin," https://www.travelwisconsin.com/article/museums-history/experience-history-the-underground-railroad-in-wisconsin; *Roots of Freedom: Underground Railroad Heritage Trail* (Racine, WI: Racine Heritage Museum, 2008), 12–13; "The Underground Railroad in Wisconsin," Wisconsin History online; Julia Pferdehirt, *Freedom Train North: Stories of the Underground Railroad in Wisconsin* (Middleton, WI: Living History Press, 1998), 6–18, 43–49; Doug Welch, *The Milton House: Interests of the Highest Value,* 2nd ed. (Castroville, TX: Black Rose Writing, 2018), 13–21, 68.

The Milton House is the only authenticated stop on the Underground Railroad in Wisconsin that currently can be toured. A historical marker located at Racine Monument Square commemorates Joshua Glover and the citizens of Racine who, at their peril, aided one of their own out of the bondage of slavery. Two murals, paid for by the State of Wisconsin, honoring Joshua Glover and Caroline Quarles are located at the site of the former Samuel Brown farm in Milwaukee.

8. Manski, "State Power against Slave Power," 15; "Wide Awakes," https:// en.wikipedia.org/wiki/Wide-Awakes; Jon Grinspan, "'Young Men for War': The Wide Awakes and Lincoln's 1860 Presidential Campaign," *Journal of American History* 96 (September 2009): 357–78.

The Norwegian Synod had in its early history a close relationship with the Missouri Synod, whose base was in a slave state. When C. F. Solberg raised the issue of the Norwegian Synod's teachings on slavery in *Emigranten*, the Synod pastors offered a Biblical interpretation that according to the Word of God, slavery was not "a sin in and of itself." The Synod got the reputation of defending slavery. C. L. Clausen and a dozen or more congregations broke with the Synod because of it.

Notes to Chapter 4

1. Maldwyn Allen Jones, *American Immigration* (Chicago: University of Chicago Press, 1960), 92–94; John Higham, *Strangers in the Land: Patterns of American Nativism, 1860–1925*, 3rd ed. (New Brunswick, NJ: Rutgers University Press, 1994), 21, 124–26; Lovoll, *The Promise of America*, 313–14; Lovoll, *A Century of Urban Life*, 89–90; "Foreign Enlistment in the American Civil War," https://en.wikipedia.org/wiki/Foreign_enlistment_in_the _American_Civil_War; William L. Burton, *Melting Pot Soldiers: The Union's Ethnic Regiments* (Ames: Iowa State University Press, 1988), vii–x.

2. *Wisconsin Blue Book: 1962*, 76, quote 76; David Herbert Donald, Jean Harvey Baker, Michael F. Holt, *The Civil War and Reconstruction* (New York: W. W. Norton & Co., 2001), 116–24; Harry Hansen, *The Civil War: A History* (New York: Penguin Books, 1961), 28–33, quotes 30, 31; Andersen, "Lincoln and the Union," 86, 87–90, 93; "1860 United States Presidential Election," https://en.wikipedia.org/wiki/1860_United_States_presidential _election; Larson, *Wisconsin and the Civil War*, 21–22; Rudolph J. Vecoli, "*Contadini* in Chicago: A Critique of *The Uprooted*," *Journal of American History* 51 (December 1964): 405–17, quote 406; Blegen, *Civil War Letters of*

Colonel Heg, 20; Emory M. Thomas, *The Confederate Nation 1861–1865* (New York: Harper Perennial, 2011), 38, 41, 64–66, 85–87, 93–94, 124, 125.

3. Bordewich, *Bound for Canaan,* 11–13, quote 13; Clint Smith, *How the Word Is Passed: A Reckoning with the History of Slavery Across America* (New York: Little, Brown and Co., 2021), prologue, back cover; *Slavery in America: The Montgomery Slave Trade* (Montgomery, AL: Equal Justice Initiative, 2018), 13, 23, 24, 55; Donald, Baker, and Holt, *The Civil War and Reconstruction,* 60–73; "Causes of the Civil War," https://www.historynet.com/causes -of-the-civil-war.

"The state of Texas had a small contingent of Norwegians in 1860, all together 321 people. By 1870 this number had increased to 552, and in 1880 there were 941 Norwegians in Texas. Most of them resided in Bosque County. . . . Norwegian men joined the confederate forces, fought for the cause of the South, and defended the right of each state to self-determination. Among the Norwegians in the South, however, the war never became a crusade, a conflict that created heroes and fired the imagination. . . . Most historians have maintained not only that Norwegians in Texas were luke-warm in their will to fight, but that a large percentage of them sided with the North and felt loyalty to the Union": Lovoll, *The Promise of America,* 109–11.

4. Burton, *Melting Pot Soldiers,* 11, 15–16, 21, 48–51, 57–58, 91, 109, 112, 113–15, 166, 169–70, quote 51; Lovoll, *The Promise of America,* 75, 107–8.

5. Jerry Rosholt, *Ole Goes to War: Men from Norway Who Fought in America's Civil War* (Decorah, IA: Vesterheim Norwegian-American Museum, 2003), 15, 20; Petter Strøm Drevland, "Norwegian Immigrants in the American Civil War: Reasons for Enlistment according to the America Letters" (Masteroppgave ved Det Humanistiske Fakultet, Universitetet i Oslo, 28,5,2013), 1, 25–46; Orm Øverland, *Immigrant Minds, American Identities: Making the United States Home, 1870–1930* (Urbana: University of Illinois Press, 2000), 7–8; Harry Cleven, "Introduction," in Ager, *Colonel Heg and His Boys,* xiv, xv, xix; "Enrollment Act," https://en.wikipedia.org/wiki/Enroll ment_Act; Karl Jakob Skarstein, *Til våpen for det nye land. Norske innvan-drere i den amerikanske borgerkrig* (Oslo: J. W. Cappelenns Forlag A.S., 2001), 75; Kenneth Carley, *Minnesota in the Civil War: An Illustrated History* (2000; St. Paul: Minnesota Historical Society Press, 2014), xvii–xix, xxv, 4–13, 78–79, 81, quotes xxv, xviii; "The Civil War (1861–1865)," Historic Fort Snelling, https://www. mnhs.org/fortsnelling/learn/military-history/civil-war; Hamp-ton Smith, "First Minnesota Volunteer Infantry Regiment," MNopedia;

Emigranten, September 16, 1861; Lovoll, *The Promise of America*, 115–16; Lovoll, *Norwegians on the Prairie*, 20–24, 40; Hans Mattson, *Reminiscences: The Story of an Emigrant* (St. Paul, MN: D. D. Merrill Company, 1892), 57–67, quote 61; *Wisconsin Blue Book: 1962*, 146–47.

On August 18, 1862, a second war broke out in Minnesota. The Dakota from their reservations along the upper Minnesota River finally vented their frustration and under the leadership of Little Crow took up arms against their white oppressors. The US–Dakota War obstructed Minnesota's Civil War engagement. There were three regular army posts on the Minnesota frontier, garrisoned by Companies B, C, and D of the Fifth Volunteer Infantry. Minnesota had responded to the call for more troops to fight in the South by organizing the Fifth, Sixth, Seventh, Eighth, Ninth, and Tenth Infantry Regiments. They were all mustering at Fort Snelling. In August they were sent west rather than south and were joined by the Third. Defeat of the Dakota in several battles had made the Third and Fifth Regiments available for reassignment to duty in the South in late 1862 and early 1863. Other regiments assigned frontier guard duty in Minnesota were later sent south as well. In the summer of 1864 the Eighth was the last regiment to be ordered south.

Gary Clayton Anderson, *Massacre in Minnesota: The Dakota War of 1862, the Most Violent Ethnic Conflict in American History* (Norman: University of Oklahoma Press, 2019), 83–111, 135–69, esp. 106–11; Lovoll, *The Promise of America*, 15, 20, 128–32; Carley, *Minnesota in the Civil War*, 78–79.

6. Larson, *Wisconsin and the Civil War*, 16–17, 23–24, 45–46, quote 23; Blegen, *Civil War Letters of Colonel Heg*, 20–22; *Emigranten*, August 26, 1861.

7. *Emigranten*, September 2, 16, 30, October 7, 14, December 23, 1861; Blegen, *Civil War Letters of Colonel Heg*, 20, 53n, quote 53; Agnes M. Larson, *John A. Johnson: An Uncommon American* (Northfield, MN: Norwegian-American Historical Association, 1969), 4–5, 24–27, 40–41, 60–61, quote 60; Johnson, *Det Skandinaviske Regiments Historie*, 15–16, quote 15; Lovoll, *The Promise of America*, 51; P. G. Dietrichson, *En kortfattet Skildring af det Femtende Wisconsin Regiments Historie og Virksomhed under Borgerkrigen* (Chicago, IL: John Andersen & Co., 1884), 6–7.

8. Blegen, *Civil War Letters of Colonel Heg*, 22–23, 24, quote 19–20; Larson, *John A. Johnson*, 42–43; *Emigranten*, September 30, October 7, 14, November 18, 1861; special number of *Emigranten* made up from the issues of October 7 and 14, 1861.

9. Blegen, *Civil War Letters of Colonel Heg*, 24, 52–53, quote 53; *Emigranten*, February 17, March 14, 21, 1862; Ager, *Colonel Heg and His Boys*, xvii, 12–13; Lovoll, *A Century of Urban Life*, 86–90; E. Biddle Heg, "Twelve Civil War Letters of Colonel Heg to His Son," *Norwegian-American Studies* 32 (1989): 179; Skarstein, *Til våpen for det nye land*, 80. Quote from *Wisconsin State Journal* translated from the Norwegian.

The Norwegian Nora Society became lodge #1 of the Order of the Knights of the White Cross (Ordenen af Riddere af det Hvide Kors) on January 27, 1863.

Notes to Chapter 5

1. James Robertson Jr., "The Brother's War," Radio IQ, August 23, 2019, https://www.wvtf.org/civil-war-series/2019-08-23/the-brothers-war; Thomas, *The Confederate Nation*, 146–47, 274: Hansen, *The Civil War*, 125–34; Ager, *Colonel Heg and His Boys*, 3–4; Donald, Baker, and Holt, *The Civil War and Reconstruction*, 199–201, quotes 199, 201; Larson, *Wisconsin and the Civil War*, 86–87; Peter Cozzens, *This Terrible Sound: The Battle of Chickamauga* (Urbana: University of Illinois Press, 1992), 323.

2. Ager, *Colonel Heg and His Boys*, xix; Blegen, *Civil War Letters of Colonel Heg*, 26–27, 150, 225, 226, quotes 27, 67, 87; Heg, "Twelve Civil War Letters of Colonel Heg to His Son," 180, 189, quote 189.

In the 1860 federal census Gunild Heg (1833–1922) is registered as Cornelia Heg. It became her name the rest of her life. Hans Heg consistently addressed his wife as Gunild, and this name will be used throughout the narrative. She spent the last years of her life in the home of her daughter, Hilda Heg Fowler, and son-in-law, former congressman Charles H. Fowler, in Elizabeth, New Jersey.

3. Rosholt, *Ole Goes to War*, 41–46; Blegen, *Civil War Letters of Colonel Heg*, 32–33, 64–65, 76, quotes 33, 65, 68, 73, 76; E. B. Quiner, *The Military History of Wisconsin: A Record of the Civil and Military Patriotism of the State* (Chicago: Clarke & Co., 1866), 615; William DeLoss Love, *Wisconsin in the War of Rebellion* (Chicago: Church and Goodman, 1866), 462, 469–74; Larson, *Wisconsin and the Civil War*, 84–87; Donald, Baker, and Holt, *The Civil War and Reconstruction*, 201–2; Ager, *Colonel Heg and His Boys*, 15–16; "Island No. 10," https://en.wikipedia.org/wiki/Battle_of_Island_Number_Ten.

4. Blegen, *Civil War Letters of Colonel Heg*, 26, 33, 34, 140–48, quotes 34, 140, 143, 147; Quiner, *Military History of Wisconsin*, 614–17, quote 616; DeLoss Love, *Wisconsin in the War of Rebellion*, 607–20, quote 616; Donald,

Baker, and Holt, *The Civil War and Reconstruction*, 357–61; Thomas, *The Confederate Nation*, 164–66; Hansen, *The Civil War*, 103–6, 109.

5. Blegen, *Civil War Letters of Colonel Heg*, 35–36, 162–70, quote 163; DeLoss Love, *Wisconsin in the War of Rebellion*, 628–36; Dietrichson, *Femtende Wisconsin Regiments Historie og Virksomhed*, 12–13; Langeland, "Oberst H. C. Heg," in Johnson, *Det Skandinaviske Regiments Historie*, 107, quote 107; Ager, *Colonel Heg and His Boys*, 159–61, 180, quote 180.

6. Blegen, *Civil War Letters of Colonel Heg*, 36, 38–46, 188–220, 221, quotes 39, 188, 204; Ira Berlin, *Slaves No More: Three Essays on Emancipation and the Civil War* (Cambridge, NY: Cambridge University Press, 1992), 4–5, 49–51, 136–37, 156–57, 178–81, 189–90; Emancipation Proclamation, https://www.archives.gov/exhibits/featured-documents/emancipation -proclamation; Quiner, *Military History of Wisconsin*, 622–25, quotes 622, 623; Ager, *Colonel Heg and His Boys*, 30–32, 54, 59, 205–9, quotes 31, 54; Colbo, "The Life Story of Colonel Hans Christian Heg," 24; Larson, *Wisconsin in the Civil War*, 98–99; Andersen, "Lincoln and the Union," 107, 119, 121; Albert Skofstad, "Last Moments of Colonel Heg," *Wisconsin State Journal*, October 27, 1863, 2; Hansen, *The Civil War*, 623–41; Cozzens, *This Terrible Sound*, 40–44, 196–229, 539–53. Heg's remains were later moved to the yard of the Norway Lutheran Church his father Even Heg erected.

7. Blegen, *Civil War Letters of Colonel Heg*, quote 43; "Chickamauga," https://www.battlefields.org/learn/civil-war/battles/chickamauga; "Johannes Johnson Thoe Letters," in Civil War Papers, NAHA, translation by the author; Quiner, *Military History of Wisconsin*, 631; Hansen, *The Civil War*, 578–611; Ager, *Colonel Heg and His Boys*, 41–42, 44–43, 48–49, 112–20, quotes 41, 43, 48; Anne J. Bailey, "Sherman's March to the Sea," New Georgia Encyclopedia; "Battle of Appomattox Court House," https://www.history .com/topics/american-civil-war/appomattox-court-house; *Emigranten*, April 17, 20, 24, 1865.

Ager, *Colonel Heg and His Boys*, on page 167, is the single source that asserts the following: "The Norwegian regiment did not take part in this battle at New Hope Church, which took place on May 25th, but the battle at Pickett's Mill five miles northeast of New Hope Church on the 27th of May."

8. William B. Hesseltine, ed., *Civil War Prisons* (Kent, OH: Kent State University Press, 1962), 5–8, quote 6; Donald, Baker, and Holt, *The Civil War and Reconstruction*, 244–46, quote 244; Buslett, *Det Femtende Regiment Wisconsin Frivillige*, 204–35; Ager, *Colonel Heg and His Boys*, 8, 141, 147–57, 164–65, quotes 148, 154; "Ole C. Johnson," 1–4, quote 3, in the Norwegian

American Genealogical Center, Madison, WI; Rosholt, *Ole Goes to War*, 48–50; Bjorn Aslakson, "Ten Months a Prisoner in Andersonville, Savannah, Millerr, Blackshire and Thomasville Confederacy Prisons," in Civil War Papers, NAHA. From Willmar, Minnesota, and in the Fifteenth, Aslakson wrote a detailed and intriguing account about his own and his fellow Fifteenth Wisconsin sufferers' experiences.

See Torbjørn Greipsland, *Nordmenn i dødsleirene* (Askim, Norway: Emigrantforlaget, 2005) for further information about Norwegian inmates in Confederate prisons. There is an English version.

9. Blegen, *Civil War Letters of Colonel Heg*, 1–2, quote 2; information about reunions from collection of Racine County Heritage Museum; program of Fifteenth Wisconsin Memorial Service in author's possession; Lovoll, *The Promise of America*, 297–98; *Morgenbladet*, June 25, 1925; *Middagsavisen*, June 25, 1825; *Aftenposten*, June 25, 1925; Julius E. Olson unveiling address, program of unveiling, in Civil War Papers, NAHA; "Hans Christian Heg," https://military-history.fandom.com/wiki/Hans_Christian _Heg; "Statue of Hans Christian Heg," https://en.wikipedia.org/wiki/Statue _of_Hans_Christian_Heg; *Wisconsin State Journal*, October 18, 1926; quote "Col. Heg Statue Rededication, Sunday 29 May 2022," program.

Waldemar Ager (1869–1941) was a gifted and original Norwegian American novelist. He was unyielding in championing Norwegian American cultural growth. He edited and for a time owned the newspaper *Reform*, in Eau Claire, Wisconsin, and edited the magazine *Kvartalskrift* (Quarterly) for the Norwegian Society.

Index

Page numbers in *italics* indicate illustrations.

Norway Township, Wisconsin, 25,
42
Norwegian American Lutheranism,
and Haugean faith, 16
Norwegian emigration to America:
and already existing communities, 30; and "America books,"
22–23, 29, 35; and "America letters," 21, 22, 29; basic facts about
founding phase (1825–65), 28,
29; deaths during voyage, 26–27;
from Drammen, 19–20, 22, 23,
25; from Lier, 25; Norwegian
settlements by eve of Civil War,
37; pattern of, 28–29, 50; propaganda against, 48; reasons for,
20–21, 24, 26, 29–30; route by
way of Gothenburg, 22, 23, 24;
from Tinn, 22, 23, 24, 26; voyage
described, 25, 27
Norwegian Evangelical Lutheran
Church of America, 64–65, 69
Norwegian immigrants: and agriculture, 33; and descendants in
Upper Midwest, 124; home-
making myth of, 124; in Iowa
(1850), 35; in Minnesota, 35, 37;
Norse-American Centennial, 7;
and Republican Party, 86–87; in
Union Army, 124, 125–26, 127–
28; in Wisconsin (1850–60),
33–34; in Wisconsin (1860), 87,
128. *See also specific settlements*
Norwegian Migration to America,
1825–1860 (Blegen), 19
Norwegian Society of America (Det
norske Selskab af Amerika), 173,
175–76

Norwegian Synod (Norwegian
Evangelical Lutheran Church of
America), 64–65, 69

"Oberst H. C. Heg" (Colonel H. C.
Heg by Langeland), 76
Ødegården, Even Hansen. *See* Heg,
Even Hansen
Old Muskego Church, 52–53,
54–56, 55, 65, 189n3
Ole Goes to War (Rosholt), 171
Olsdatter, Gunhild, 18–19
Olsen, Jakob, 18, 19
Olson, Even E., 191n8
Olson, Ivar, 167
Olson, Julius E., 177
"Opposing Forces in the Chickam-
auga Campaign" (Cozzens), 158
Order of the Knights of the White
Cross (Ordenen af Riddere af det
Hvide Kors), 197n9
Øverland, Orm, 124

Pedersen, Daniel, 167
Peerson, Cleng, 20
Perryville, Battle of, 143, 149,
150–52
Pickett, George E., 127
Pickett's Mill, Battle of, 198n7
press (immigrant): German, 128;
importance of, 65–66; Norwegian American, 67, 69, 161–62,
168; as political organs, 66,
86–87, 90, 115, 116; Scandinavian
joint organ, 190n5. *See also*
individual newspapers
Preus, A. C., 63–64, 70
Preus, H. A., 64, 70

Professor emeritus of history at St. Olaf College, Odd S. Lovoll is the author of several books on the Norwegian American immigrant experience, among them *Norwegians on the Prairie*, *Norwegian Newspapers in America*, and *Across the Deep Blue Sea*.